"*Millennial Money Makeover* changes the conversation around finances by providing a relatable, understandable and immediately actionable plan to better your finances today and in the future!"

—Matt Reiner, CFA, CFP®, CEO and cofounder of Wela and author of *Ready to be Rich*

"Do you control your money or does your money control you? *Millennial Money Makeover* provides timeless practical advice for the world's next major generational economic force. This book will both motivate and guide you to immediately find ways to better yourself and the world around you!"

—Noah Barsky, PhD, CPA, professor, Villanova University School of Business (USA)

MILLENNIAL
MONEY
MAKEOVER

Escape Debt, Save for Your Future,
and Live the Rich Life Now

CONOR RICHARDSON

**CAREER
PRESS**

This edition first published in 2019 by Career Press,
an imprint of Red Wheel/Weiser, LLC
With offices at:
65 Parker Street, Suite 7
Newburyport, MA 01950
www.redwheelweiser.com
www.careerpress.com

ISBN: 978-1-63265-145-7
Library of Congress Cataloging-in-Publication Data
available upon request.

Cover design by Laura Beers
Cover art courtesy of iStock
Interior photos/images by Conor Richardson
Interior by Gina Schenck
Typeset in Minion Pro and DIN OT

Printed in Canada
MAR
10 9 8 7 6 5 4 3 2 1

To my wife, Kristen, for your unwavering love and support.
And to Augustus, so that you may understand.

"Yes, there are two paths you can go by,
But in the long run,
There's still time to change the road you're on."

—Robert Plant and Jimmy Page

Contents

Introduction:
The Millennial's Way

This book was an accident.

A calamity of errors in my mid twenties forced me to make major financial changes in my life. These changes didn't happen overnight, but were a slow accumulation of real-world education, action, and determination. And the only way for me to deal with these changes was to write about them. The widening gap between where I wanted to be financially and the reality of my financial position produced an inescapable internal battle, one that I chose to fight. Something was fundamentally wrong with my finances, and I knew it.

My exasperation eventually forced me to examine my finances as a whole, and I came to the sudden realization that I needed a financial makeover. At that moment, I decided to completely overhaul how I thought about money.

If you are reading this book, the chances are that you are feeling some similar sentiments. Let me take a guess: You are living paycheck to paycheck, you have credit card debt, you have student loans to pay off, your savings are laughable, and you wince at the term "401(k)." You understand that you are behind.

This is how I felt too. How far behind exactly, I didn't know. What I did know was that I was going to stop living on the edge of financial collapse. Luckily, as a certified public accountant (CPA) I was educated with the tools for financial success.

Armed with an abundance of classroom knowledge, I was working in the world's financial capital, New York City, but disregarding any financial prudence. Instead of focusing on fixing my finances and building my wealth (like I knew that I should be), I was scrambling to get by, trying to keep up with the Joneses, and ignoring my savings.

In other words, I was feeling very American.

After several years of working hard, with virtually nothing to show for it, I decided to make a change and turn professional with my money; once I did this, I was on the path to the rich life. After that critical decision my life changed for the better, and I discovered the secrets of the wealthy. That is what I want to share with you in this book.

My money makeover started when I decided to take hold of my future and learn everything I could about money. Stuck in a situation that was not producing what I wanted, I chose to *redirect* my life and head in the right direction. You can too. There is *always* time to change the road you are on.

The six-step program laid out in this book will take you from being a broke Millennial to a rich Millennial. How fast that happens is up to you. By eliminating debt, creating a budget, learning how to buy big-ticket items, and saving for the future you will finally start to dominate your finances.

You are blessed with choices every day. Make the decision today that you are going to achieve financial greatness and enter the money makeover. The six-step program in this book helped to change my life, and I guarantee it will change yours too.

Let's get going.

The New Normal: WTF

There seems to be an element of inevitability in the way our lives play out. The success sequence of previous generations—spouse, house, kids, and lifelong careers—is broken. The slow decay of this success sequence has crept its way into our daily life, and by osmosis, our financial expectations. A collision of economic and cultural systemic problems has reached a tipping point, brought on by stagnant incomes, exacerbating credit card debt, astronomical student loans, ridiculous housing prices, and low retirement savings. These trends have sadly become the new normal, especially for Millennials.

Researchers are beginning to notice. In a fascinating study, Annamaria Lusardi, a professor at The George Washington University School of Business, investigated the financial consistency of young Americans between the ages of twenty-three and thirty-five years old. With more than 5,500 observations, the study revealed significant findings among young people, including their attitudes toward finances and apparent inability to handle them.

- Seventy-six percent of Millennials are financially illiterate.
- Sixty-four percent of Millennials do not have a retirement account.

- Fifty-four percent of Millennials are concerned about their ability to repay student loans.

- Fifty-two percent of Millennials are unhappy about their financial situation.[1]

Think about those statistics for a second. Seriously, let them sink it.

As one of the largest and most diverse generations in US history, Millennials will make a significant impact on the United States. As a highly educated, optimistic, and ethnically diverse group of people, we consist of millions of young adults born between the late 1970s and the mid-1990s. With confidence on our side, we are able and willing to take on the economic challenges of our time, even after the Great Recession of 2008.

The problem is, Millennials face unprecedented financial hurdles, which has researchers worried. Says Annamaria Lusardi, "Looking at the data from the most recent National Financial Capability Study, we are concerned about their unprecedented levels of student debt and their overconfidence in financial matters."[2] In other words, Millennials face a challenge that we are overconfident we can eliminate. This presents a major problem.

As the brilliant English physicist Stephen Hawking said, "The greatest enemy of knowledge is not ignorance, it is the illusion of knowledge."[3] Overconfidence has the tendency to put blinders on the greatest of us, and when this overconfidence deals in matters with which we are unfamiliar, such as how to handle our money (clearly demonstrated in Lusardi's study), the results can be catastrophic.

There is good news though. Millennials are avid learners, and we understand there is always more to learn. This is particularly true with money. If we want to dig ourselves out of this hole and progress toward the life we want, it must begin with action. You do *not* have to shoulder the burdens of the *new normal*. After all, who the hell wants to be normal?

Getting Unstuck

Starting anything new can be challenging. When confronted with the option of something new or better, people often refer to the status quo. As we saw earlier, the status quo puts people in an incredibly unhealthy financial position. It leaves people feeling stuck and burdened. And the only way to move forward, the way toward progress and promise, is to get unstuck.

The act of getting unstuck starts when you leave all your previous excuses behind. Own everything about your finances and do not fall prey to the typical excuses:

- I don't know where to begin.
- Nobody taught me this in school.
- This debt isn't my fault.
- Money is not really my thing.

Transforming your relationship with money shouldn't be difficult. Yes, it will require some work, but learning to manage your money and your financial life will not be an intellectually taxing experience, only a test of determination.

If you allow it, money can be your best friend. Money is awesomely flexible, hardworking, diligent, and loyal. What people *perceive* to be hard about money is their *behavior* with money.

Living the rich life is not as advertised on television. The rich life requires a dedicated focus and a new kind of behavior with money. The rich life requires keeping money around, not giving it away. The rich life involves putting money to work instead of letting it remain idle. The rich life involves progress and moving forward. The rich life starts with getting unstuck.

Things Rich People Know

The rich think differently. They know the secrets of life that have unlocked their ability to eradicate debt and put their money to work. They have an uncanny ability to decipher the important elements of any major financial transaction. They think deeply about how and when to make big purchases, and they question their emotions and assumptions before making major financial decisions. When doing all of this, rich people use the following rules to guide them toward success:

- *Focus on big wins:* Working hard is not always the answer. Working hard on the right things is how the elite compete. There will be areas in your financial life that disproportionately affect your chances of achieving financial success. Hone in on these big items and dedicate yourself to tackling them with tenacity.

- *Action always beats inaction:* Do I start paying off my student loans today? Do I start investing more now? Instead of plaguing themselves with doubt, rich people know that if you are asking yourself these questions, the answer is inevitable: Yes! Do. Act. Make decisions. The momentum of action will propel you forward.

- *Intangible goods are often the greatest in value:* The rich life is about finding lasting and meaningful things. Intangibles, like having the financial freedom to make a career change or take a year off to travel, are much more rewarding than a quickly depreciating asset. Graduates of the money makeover understand that the value of intangibles outlasts the quick rush of tangible purchases.

- *Delayed gratification always trumps immediate gratification:* Whenever the moment lures you into the ephemeral hands of immediate gratification, resist. Cheap wins and quick rewards come at the cost of long-term gains and progress. The learned behavior of resisting impulse purchases is often the strongest predictor of success.

The Quickest Way to Get Rich

If you want to be rich, then act rich.

Most Americans behave in precisely the opposite manner. They have a warped mental image of "the rich life" fueled by too much television and social media. I have a name for this perception: "the filtered life." It distorts everything.

The filtered life involves items of extreme luxury being flaunted as everyday experiences, such as fancy cars, expensive jewelry, constant travel, and giant houses. This level of consumption leaves the rest of us scratching our heads, wondering what we are doing wrong. It should come as no surprise that most people correlate this type of hyper-spending with wealth. Nothing could be further from the truth.

The typical American millionaire does not act like a Kardashian. Instead, these millionaires lead a profoundly unsexy and frugal lifestyle. They typically do not spend lots of money on suits, watches, or other nonproductive purchases. In fact, in the groundbreaking book *The Millionaire Next*

Door, authors Thomas Stanley and William Danko reveal that more than half of American millionaires have never paid more than $140 for shoes, $235 for a wristwatch, or $400 for a suit.[4] Then why does the media continue to push images of wealth and consumption in today's society? Because it is sexy, and sex always sells.

Being unsexy, however, is the quickest way to get rich. But do not just take it from me. If you want to be rich, then you should focus on the words of billionaire venture capitalist Chris Sacca, who told *Entrepreneur* magazine, "My best piece of advice for the quickest way to get rich is to not spend any of your money." Additionally, Sacca noted, "People get out ahead of themselves in debt with spending on all of their desires."[5]

This simple, yet profound, point highlights a major problem: The financial hurdles we face are often created by our actions. As Americans, we tend to acquire debt and thereby encumber our path to wealth.

Sacca also touches on one of the most fortified routes to the rich life: living well below your means. Staying out of debt, downsizing your lifestyle, and earning more money will allow you to accumulate savings at an exponential rate. The formula is proven. And once you start making your money work for you, instead of you working for your money, you will understand what being wealthy truly means.

The Millennial Money Makeover

It is time to hit the reset button. Start over. Begin again.

The problem is that you were not taught much about personal finances in school. Even as a CPA, I didn't receive this knowledge in my formal education. It wasn't until I started living in the real world that I learned how to master my money.

Not many people have been shown the path to success. Everyone is focused on the result of being wealthy, having money to spend, but not the process itself. Consequently, few people adopt the right habits, hacks, and rules to increase their wealth quickly. Financial freedom can be engineered. And I will show you how.

If you want to turn around your finances, then start the Millennial Money Makeover. Adopting this mental outlook and way of life will pay for itself tenfold and also give you:

- Higher self-confidence
- Enhanced decision-making
- Increased career choices
- More power
- Financial freedom

The prescription for lifelong financial success can be attained by anyone. If you have the determination to be a financial rock star, then take control of your financial life.

Decide to begin your money makeover today.

Principles of Success

Millennial Money Makeover is built on the fundamental belief that everyone can turn around their finances and lead the rich life. To achieve that goal, a foundation in money principles is critical for long-term success.

The following list is a set of guiding principles to help you stay the course. They are not bound by time, location, or station. You can lean on these principles whenever you feel tempted to purchase beyond your means or question whether you are making the correct financial decision. These principles are forged in the crucible of modern Millennial life. They serve as a constant force in the swirling wind of fickle financial advice. Keep them close and read them often.

MILLENNIAL MONEY MAKEOVER PRINCIPLES OF SUCCESS

1. One rich decision wins the day.
2. Thinking big makes you win big.
3. Cash is forever king.
4. Education is continuous.
5. Debt is not a necessary evil.
6. Learning from experience is too slow.
7. Investing means you are winning.
8. Time is always on your side.
9. Technology is meant to be leveraged.
10. The rich life is about more than money.

You will find these principles selectively scattered throughout this book. They are placed in key areas to reinforce the mindset that you have the power to control your financial future. Follow these principles, and they will be integrated into the fabric of your daily financial habits.

Life is a collection of small decisions, and you have made an important one today. Dive in completely and embrace the full money makeover.

What This Book Will Teach You

This book will teach you about yourself.

You will learn that you have everything it takes to master your money and live the life you have always wanted. It will teach you that you have more willpower than you think and that deep within you a change is already taking place. The money makeover will change your financial outlook forever.

All you have to do is follow a simple step-by-step sequence that will build up your riches and set you up for lifelong financial success.

In this book, you will learn the six steps to turn your finances around and gain true wealth.

1. Decide to change your relationship with money and turn professional. This is where your makeover begins.

2. Pay off all of your debt, including credit cards and student loans, as soon as possible. The secret is in the process.

3. Learn how and when to start budgeting and the importance of laying down a path to follow. Building your plan to the rich life will expedite your collision with success.

4. Become an expert on the three biggest purchases made early in life and understand how to crush them, makeover style.

5. Set up the necessary savings, investment, and retirement accounts to learn how to accumulate wealth. Putting your money to work allows you to do more of the things you love.

6. Construct the perfect automated money flow system and leverage technology. Sitting back and watching your money pour into your accounts, without having to lift a finger, is priceless.

This book is jam-packed with information from entrepreneurs, authors, and professors about how to become prepared for any financial situation. This book will teach you all that you need to know about interest rates, how to pay off debt insanely fast, the proper way to invest, the best way to buy a house, and countless other secrets of the wealthy.

The secret to getting rich is out. With a dedicated focus and willingness to follow the money makeover, anyone can be a financial success. The money makeover begins with a decision—one that you have already made.

1

A Rich Decision: Make the Choice to Understand Your Money

Decision is the ultimate power.
—Tony Robbins

If you want to find out the meaning of life, go to New York City.

When I was twenty-eight years old, I had a life-changing moment that would alter the trajectory of my life. Some would call it an epiphany, others a financial wake-up call. I call it a financial awakening.

In the fall of 2014, I was living in New York and enjoying every minute. My career was taking off, I was making lifelong friendships, and I was continuously learning. Life was perfect.

New York taught me about life, the minimum viable space for an apartment, the art of navigating crowded subways, how to hail a taxi, and the value of work. With a city that eats up most of a young professional's budget with rent, it also taught me how to survive on a small amount of discretionary income. Allocating my spending was crucial to survival, and as a result, savings was always a second thought, if a thought at all.

But one evening everything came crashing down. For some reason, I decided that I wanted to start saving more—well, really, just save at *all*. I was getting sick of just getting by every month. Something inside me was saying there was more to life than living paycheck to paycheck. So I sat down at my desk in my fifth-floor walk-up apartment, overlooking Brooklyn, and put together my first *real* budget.

That is when the clouds parted.

As a newly minted certified public accountant (CPA), I lived in Excel most of my days and nights. Creating financial projections for existing businesses, models for business plans, and slicing through mounds of data were routine projects. But modeling out my *own* future and thinking about the business of "*me*" always seemed to fall to the bottom of the to-do list. I decided to change that by sitting down to figure out exactly where I stood.

The result was not pretty. My financial life was in shambles. If I was going to save myself, I knew that I needed to do something quick and drastic. At that moment, I decided to change. I decided to change my relationship with money forever and turn professional with my finances. That is when my money makeover began.

Something tells me you are looking to do the same.

That evening is seared into my mind as one of the most transformational moments of my life. It was a moment of full decision. I was going to stop. I was going to stop living on the edge. I was going to stop unnecessarily spending on clothes, trips, and going out with friends. And I was going to stop living in New York, the city I loved. My financial life was a wreck, and the only way to fix it was with a complete money makeover.

This will happen to you too. Perhaps it already has. There will come a time when you realize you are losing control of your finances and everything isn't quite working out. You will become tired of the routine—fighting through the Sunday Scaries, hating Mondays, living for the weekend, and haphazardly spending money. When you finally become fatigued by it all, you will know it is time for a change.

Perhaps that is why you picked up this book?

I changed my life during my late twenties, but only after I dusted off the haze of the previous years. If I remained entrenched in my old routine, I realized my long-term financial outlook was bleak. If, on the other hand, I wanted the financial freedom that I had always dreamed of, then I was going to have to make major changes in my life. The dormant need to take control of my life was beginning to wake up. It was time for a money makeover.

When we first start our careers, all we know about money is that we do not have enough of it. And far too often, we are naive to the fact that creating a solid financial base in our twenties and thirties will pave the way to lifelong financial success. Our distraction is not without merit. As young professionals, we are perpetually engrossed with the mythology of the success sequence: trying to find the right job, the right spouse, and just generally working things out.

We tend to become overwhelmed with life's expenses, and as a result, we are always stressed about money. The comforting news is that you are not alone. Nearly 70 percent of Millennials report feeling financially stressed.[1] Making the choice today to get your finances in order can alleviate this burdensome stress and increase your happiness.

If you are merely starting to think about paying off your debt, saving, or developing a financial plan, this book will guide you on your way to financial success. This book will help you set up the financial ecosystem to create lasting change. You will finally be on your way to financial freedom.

Sounds great, right? Well, there is one catch. The steps in this book will present the agenda for success. But as it is with most difficult decisions in life, change can only begin with you *taking action*. Picking up the phone to call your credit card companies, setting up your savings account, opening retirement accounts, and automating your finances will all have to be done on your time and by the work of your own hands.

Turning Professional

Let this moment be one that you remember. Realize that this is a unique opportunity. You have the chance for a complete transformation—to escape debt, build up savings, create a career that matters, and live life on your own terms.

Take the time today to consciously decide that you are going to turn professional in your finances. This will be one of the most important decisions you will ever make. Commit to leading an exceptional life in which you can buy your dream car and purchase that perfect house.

"I could divide my life into two parts: before turning pro and after. After is better."
—Steven Pressfield, *Turning Pro*

The concept of living a financially healthy lifestyle is not novel. It is, however, a very hard thing to accomplish in today's society. We live in a world in which we are perpetually inundated with marketing campaigns designed to pull us away from being financially prudent. The competing messages are everywhere: *Buy this fancy new purse. Don't you need that new shirt? Do you have the latest iPhone?* We are constantly reminded of our inferiority if we do not have the appropriate *stuff*. Ignore those voices and listen to the one in your head (that would be me right now). You do not need excess, and you do not need more. Look around you; you barely use what you already own (more on this in Chapter 3).

A money makeover starts with the realization that you are an incredibly important person. Mastering your money is worth every minute of your time. You need to recognize that only you control your financial destiny.

This book is here to help as a financial tool. As humans, we are hardwired to use the tools around us to construct our environment. Use this tool to better your life. In this book, you have the insights and perspectives of those who have gone before you. They are adamantly showing you the path to success. Live a debt-free life. Invest when everyone else is spending. Create the income to last a lifetime. When you start to get uncomfortable, that is when you know you are beginning to get close. Launch yourself, and your finances, forward.

It is the few who end up on the path to success, but there is always time to change the road you are on.

Turn professional today.

....

Millennial Money Makeover Principle of Success: One Rich Decision Wins the Day

Making the decision to turn professional with your money will change the trajectory of your life. Absorbing this principle will increase your appetite for change.

....

Building Your Confidence

Stop deferring action to the future. *Do I need to pay that bill today? Can I just make the minimum payment? Should I make my student loan payment this month?* One reason why people procrastinate when it comes to making hard choices is fear. Fear that they will have to change. Fear that they may be socially excluded from the tribe. Fear that they will be wrong. This fear causes paralysis and fuels the status quo.

Fear is public enemy number one.

> *"Skill and confidence are an unconquered army."*
> —George Herbert

The good news is that fear can be beaten. Fear ushers in negative thoughts, which lead to negative actions or inaction. The best way to beat fear is by *confidence-building*. By replacing your negative thoughts with positive and *confidence-building* thoughts, the cycle of fear can be broken. Our brains are remarkably powerful, and if you train your brain to harness the power of positive thinking, remarkable changes begin to unfold.

One of the secrets of the rich life is: Confidence is a commodity. Confidence can be developed, mined, and acquired over time. By practicing confidence-building techniques, you can produce confidence to be used at your convenience. This confidence will permeate all aspects of your life, including your career, personal relationships, and money management.

The following list displays fears people face when failing to realize their financial potential. Read the fears and their associated confidence-building responses out loud. You can download a spreadsheet with blank responses at Millennial MoneyMakeover.com

Typical Fears	Your Confident Response
Fear of feeling overwhelmed	*I am going to use this book and all of the tools in it as a resource to answer my most pressing financial questions.*
Fear of the unknown	*I am going to venture into the land of the unknown with confidence, knowing that I can conquer anything I put my mind to.*
Fear of making a mistake	*I am going to start now and make mistakes early. I will learn from them and grow.*
Fear of being poor	*I understand that living in debt sucks. I am going to turn my negative into a positive.*
Fear of making a bad investment	*All investment is good. Whether I am learning or making money, the fact that I am investing means I am winning.*

Do you feel that? That is confidence beginning to flow through your veins.

A history of poor financial decisions can lead someone to think they cannot master their finances. You do not lack ability, only knowledge that you will acquire shortly. But fear is a nasty little emotion that feeds on itself. The fear that is developed through constant debt and living a financially poor life is proliferated by a lack of three major aspects to success: autonomy, mastery, and purpose.

Popularized by Daniel Pink in his bestselling book *Drive,* these three aspects of success harness the power to gain fulfillment in most of life's endeavors.[2] Attain these three qualities in your financial life, and you will regain control of your future. Let's take a look at each one.

Autonomy

Financial autonomy, or the freedom from external control, gives you the ability to break free from dependence upon your next paycheck. If you decide that you want to quit living what I call the "just in time" paycheck lifestyle, then you need to change your relationship with money. That starts by keeping money around instead of giving it away.

What constitutes financial autonomy? When you have no debts to repay, that is financial autonomy. When you have enough savings to take a year off, that is financial autonomy. When your investments produce a secondary income stream, that is financial autonomy. Financial autonomy gives you the freedom to choose what you want to do in life. It liberates you. Maybe you finally want to start traveling or explore a new career. Whatever your reason, autonomy gives you the freedom to make choices. But *you* have to choose financial autonomy first.

Mastery

Mastery produces a kind of pride and passion. Lack of mastery, however, makes us nervous and fearful. When it comes to mastering money, most people run in the opposite direction.

There seems to be an infinite number of choices about what to do with your money. Confusion about what to do induces financial paralysis. Amid the cacophony of advice, we have been erroneously conditioned to think we need to know everything about money. The steps and principles in this book will give you all that you need to know.

Mastering your money is a necessary part of your self-education. Luckily, it only requires middle school–level math skills and an appetite for change. During your flight into financial fluency, keep the words of the Stoic philosopher Epictetus in mind: "Only the educated are free."[3]

Purpose

Developing yourself, and your finances, allows you to pursue your purpose in life. You are called to do something wonderful. For some this means teaching, starting a new business, or founding a charity.

Purpose is the deep urge you feel toward your life's work. It means finding your passion and pursuing it relentlessly. But purpose needs room to germinate. Whether your passion is philanthropy, art, writing, or business, financial stability lets you do more of what you love. Financial stability lets you find your purpose.

....

Confidence-building is a decision that we make every day. You will have to remind yourself of that continuously because the financial system is designed to decrease your confidence. But there are no recurring fees to be made on the financially intelligent. Understand that there is a lot of useless information about money and finances out there. By aiming to achieve financial autonomy, mastery, and purpose, you can hone your financial acumen. You can learn to surgically remove the useless information and decipher what is important. This process is the key to confidence-building.

The Path of Least Resistance

In recent years, technology has democratized access to information, and the former gatekeepers are slowly fading away. The market for financial advice is now saturated with opinions and overwhelming amounts of information. With the age of information asymmetry officially behind us, no one has stopped to ask if that is a good thing. It turns out, this new onslaught of information overload can actually begin to work against you.

There seems to be an infinite amount of choices about what to do with your money: options, stocks, warrants, investment properties, bonds, high-yield investments, and dividends. The terms and options seem endless. The information overload begins working against you, and you get stuck. There are just too many choices. Instead of making a decision, you simply do nothing, but find yourself yearning for a path to follow. That lack of financial action comes from an internal conundrum called *the paradox of choice.*

Marc Cuban, billionaire investor and outspoken owner of the Dallas Mavericks, has mastered this concept. Cuban has had tremendous success in business, and one of Cuban's core mantras, although initially counterintuitive, is that businesses should offer fewer options to customers, not more. Offering the path of least resistance to customers, which means fewer options, he says, "is a lesson in basic business."

In his 2011 book *How to Win at the Sport of Business,* Cuban details the debate between two schools of thought in the advertising and television universe in the early 2000s: Is it better to offer unlimited channels or suggestive programing to customers?

> Others seem to think that unlimited choice is the holy grail of TV. It's not. The reason it's not is that it's too

much work to page through an unlimited number of options. It's too much work to have to think of what it is we might like to watch. We are afraid we might miss something that we really want to watch. . . . The smart on-demand providers will present their programming guide more like Amazon.com and Netflix.com, both of which do a great job of "suggestive programming."[4]

This phenomenon of suggestive programming harnesses the power of the paradox of choice or the concept that customers may choose nothing when confronted with too many options. So reducing choice can significantly reduce anxiety for customers. As it turns out, this has a profound effect on how customers feel when they shop. For big business, limiting choices can mean increasing the bottom line. The same is true for you.

Aside from Cuban's business instinct, the paradox of choice is also grounded in social psychology and behavioral economics. Columbia University's Cheena Iyengar and Stanford University's Mark Lepper set out to examine how potential customers would react to varying degrees of choice. To do this, they set up booths outside an upscale grocery store in northern California and tried selling jam.

During the first week of the experiment, the researchers offered prospective customers a display of twenty-four varieties of jams. Then, a week later they set up shop again, but this time they only offered customers six varieties of jams. As you might have guessed, more people stopped by the first booth with the greater number of options than the second booth with fewer options. But when researchers examined the sales data, they found a peculiar occurrence: Only 3 percent of customers made a purchase from the booth containing twenty-four varieties of jam. This contrasted with the 30 percent who bought jam from the booth containing only six varieties of jam.[5]

This proved a valuable lesson: Less was more.

With all of the noise in our daily lives—work, Instagram, family—getting people to stop and concentrate on one task is becoming increasingly difficult. In our attention-driven economy, giving people the best options quickly can be the difference between success and failure. That is precisely what you will get throughout this book.

The money makeover is designed to walk you through *exactly* what you need to create a healthy financial ecosystem. Think of this program as the path of least resistance, or your *suggestive financial programming*. Ignore the advice of pundits or talking heads when it comes to finance. They generally offer horrible advice (unless, of course, they are recommending this book).

Money is easy to master, and I am going to show you exactly how to master it. You will be able to slice your way through the noise and finally achieve your financial goals. The path is here for anyone to take.

It May Get Harder Before It Gets Easier

The suggested course you are now on (reading this book) is the path less traveled. You are trying to do something that most people never accomplish in life. This will require learning the language of money, good financial behaviors, and confidence-mining techniques.

As with absorbing anything new, there will be a period of time where your skills may become *worse* than when you first started. Then, over time, your skills will gradually improve, and you start the ascent up the learning curve and go on to achieve mastery (remember Daniel Pink). According to Seth Godin, marketing expert and author of *The Dip*, rewards flow disproportionately to those who achieve mastery.[6] So why not reap the rewards?

In economics, this concept is known as the "J-Curve." Its application can be seen across some of the most sophisticated industries including private investment, global trade, biotechnology, and personal finance.

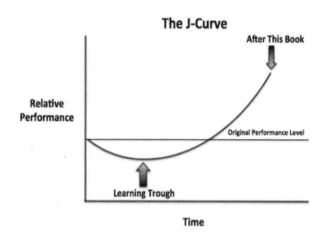

The J-Curve

The initial outlay of time and energy is followed by a dip into the learning trough. This type of downward learning is what Josh Waitzkin, world champion chess player and author of *The Art of Learning*, calls "investment in loss."[7] This early investment is a necessary step to internalize the fundamentals of whatever skill you are trying to acquire. In your case, you are trying to master money. Internalize all of the concepts in the next several chapters, and before you know it, you will be on your way up the learning curve.

Many people descend into the learning trough never to resurface. Don't let that be you. The people who devote themselves to the process and embrace the learning eventually begin to absorb the concepts they are studying. Model yourself after Waitzkin, who used this concept to become a National Master in chess and a world champion in Tai Chi push hands, conquering wildly different skills.

Learning successful financial habits will help you build the life you want. While in the throes of learning, you may be tempted to abandon your commitment to sound personal finance. Remember, it may take losing in the beginning to learn the lessons of success. This is your tuition into the university of knowledge. And if you find yourself getting frustrated, remember the J-curve. If it is hard now, easy is just around the corner.

Why Talking to Yourself Is Okay (for Now)

Shay Carl talks to himself. And he laughs at himself in the mirror too. For the thirty-something YouTube extraordinaire, this was a necessary part of his routine.

In an interview with angel investor and author Tim Ferris, Carl reveals that he used to intentionally laugh at himself in the mirror to increase his happiness. He was trying to harness the power of positive psychology and make himself feel physically better before beginning his YouTube videos. Carl had this crazy idea that if he could make himself feel happier, it would translate to his YouTube audience. And translate it did. Carl turned himself into a YouTube celebrity, and his channel has more than two billion views.[8]

Carl began his YouTube career in the midst of a midlife crisis. On the verge of a mental breakdown and sick of working his day labor job, Carl decided to change his life. As a means of coping with his newfound anxiety, Carl filmed himself, and sometimes his family, every single day for 365 days until fame came his way. He literally laughed his way to success.

For that transformative year, Shay Carl showed up every day. You need to show up every day too. The numbing routine of daily life keeps most people from achieving success. But you are not most people.

Talk to yourself in a positive light and laugh your way to success, just like Shay Carl. Use the proven positive psychological benefits of interrogative self-talk, which is a method of asking yourself pointed questions that force you to search inward. For example, a great way to kick off your day when confronted with a challenge might be, "Can I do this?" Remarkably, when you begin asking yourself questions out loud, your mind turns inward for answers, and they are always there.

Ask yourself the right question, and you just might find you already have the answer. Getting your debts paid off, building savings, and learning how to optimize your finances will take a dedicated focus.

Do you have what it takes?

Breaking the Habit Loop

In everyday life, people make huge financial decisions without giving them much thought. Sometimes, if we think the decision—what college to attend, how to pay for graduate school, or buying a home—is significant enough, we consult with family and friends. The problem is that our family and friends enthusiastically support what they *think* we want to hear, not what we *need* to hear.

This is especially true when it comes to money.

In many households, discussions about finances and money remain taboo. Discussing real-world financial topics, such as student loans, financing a new car, or securing your first mortgage, can bring to light hard economic truths about your situation. We never seek objective advice; instead, we rely on family and friends who are invested in our personal story to tell us what we want to hear. We look for affirmation, which they gladly provide. As a result, many people make horrible financial choices very early in life because they do not receive proper counsel. Well, not anymore. Consider the old paradigm broken.

> *"Make good habits and they will make you."*
> —Parks Cousins

The lack of communication around critical and expensive decisions creates a cycle of bad behavior. This cycle leads to a repetition of crucial financial errors made early in life by millions of Millennials. Our lack of communication is a bad habit that society needs to break.

In his groundbreaking book *The Power of Habit,* author Charles Duhigg discusses how habits work and describes them through the "habit loop."

The habit loop consists of a cue, followed by a routine, and finally a reward.[9] Let's take a look at our society and the current habit loop associated with discussing money. The habit loop begins with the cue to discuss some particular personal finance matter, which is demonstrated in the following example.

The Habit Loop

Jenny is a recent college graduate and has started her marketing career as a junior account executive. Earning a salary of $50,000, Jenny decides she wants to buy her dream car, a BMW. Jenny believes this car will show her family and friends she is responsible, successful, and ready to take this whole "adulting" thing seriously. But before Jenny heads to the local BMW dealership, she decides to ask her parents for some advice about her new purchase.

Jenny: *Mom and Dad, I want this new 2018 BMW 328i. I am so excited to get it (Jenny pulls out her phone to show her parents pictures of the car). Doesn't it look awesome?*

Mom: *Wow, that is cool. But buying a new car is a big decision, Jenny.*

Dad: *Jenny, I love BMWs. That's why I have the X5. BMWs are pretty expensive though. Good for you.*

That is typically where the conversation ends. Jenny's general inquiry, the cue, is met with a routine of nondiscussion. This avoidance of difficult topics is often accompanied by deflecting phrases such as:

- "That is a big decision!"
- "You should talk to a financial advisor about that!"
- "Are you sure you can afford it?"

These indifferent statements do not help anybody and are intended to spur the habit loop to its final phase, reward. In this case, the reward is moving on to another topic of conversation or perhaps washing the dishes or doing the laundry. It seems people will do anything to avoid hard discussions. Why is this? The reason is because everyone around you is invested in your success.

No one wants to tell Jenny that buying a new BMW right out of college is a horrible financial decision (see Chapter 4). Instead, they want her to be "happy." The outcomes of hard discussions can be a bitter pill to swallow and are often deferred to someone outside the family and friends circle—typically, the student loan-lending officer, the mortgage broker, or the financial advisor. The problem is that these people don't have a real responsibility to help you.

That's where this book comes in. I am not invested in your "happiness." Instead, I am invested in your *financial success*. I want you to be able to pay off your credit cards, get rid of your student loans, buy your first car, invest in income-generating assets, save for retirement, and eventually buy your first house. I want all of that for you. But we are here to have that awkward conversation of what makes good financial sense. We will have a conversation of substance about your financial fitness.

The power of habit can be deceptively strong. So, first things first, we are going to break the old habit loop. Instead of *not* talking about finances, we are going to discuss all the major financial decisions you will make. We are going to dive into how much to invest, when to pay off your credit cards, and how to build a financial future that will make you proud.

The key to getting on the right track is to create new and productive habits. This means a complete makeover to your current way of thinking and acting. Adding in positive habits and subtracting negatives habits will help you navigate the daily churn of distractions. The formula might take a moment to get used to, but once you adopt this new process, talking about money will become fun. You will have created an entirely new and healthy financial habit.

Why Setting Goals Makes You Win

Getting started, or unstuck, is often the biggest hurdle to success. But once you start to generate momentum, creating and achieving goals is fantastically important for sustained success. Goalsetting fertilizes the seed to your success because it bridges where you are today with where you want to be in the future. Goals give you a tangible and measurable path to follow.

Let's turn to an iconic Olympic champion, Michael Phelps. Throughout the course of his star-studded fifteen-year career, Phelps won twenty-three gold medals, three silver medals, and two bronze medals. His twenty-eight Olympic medals make Phelps the most decorated Olympian of all time.[10]

How did Phelps achieve such greatness? He set goals for himself very early in his career and remained adamant about meeting them. In fact, at the mature age of fifteen, Phelps already wanted to compete in the Olympics. He set that as a long-term goal and made it a reality. When asked how he approaches his goals, Phelps says "day-by-day." That should be your approach too.[11]

"He that would have fruit must climb the tree."
—Thomas Fuller

As you can see, setting goals is extremely important because it gives you a clear path on the road to success. Whether it is waking up at 5:00 a.m. to head to the pool for a workout or posting a daily YouTube video, achieving small wins will propel you toward your larger goals.

When you set goals, you unleash one of the human mind's most powerful tools, the subconscious. Even when you are unaware, your subconscious mind will begin to internalize your goals and build a deep current of thought that pulls you toward ultimately achieving your goals.

Setting goals can take you on a wild ride to success, but it all starts with laying the foundation of mapping out where you want to go. As humans, we are engineered to achieve. Sit down right now and think about your short-term and long-term goals. These could range anywhere from paying off a student loan or saving up for a down payment on your dream house. Spend time formulating a strategy for your future and develop a winning plan. Take a look at the following chart to gain inspiration for your own desired accomplishments. Go to MillennialMoneyMakeover.com to download your own goal-setting spreadsheet.

Goal Time Frame	Desired Financial Accomplishment
In three months . . .	*I will have done all of the preparation to get my finances in order.*
In six months . . .	*I will have all my credit cards paid off.*
In one year . . .	*I will have saved at least $3,000 for an emergency fund.*
In three years . . .	*I will have maxed out my annual 401(k) contribution limit and company match.*
In five years . . .	*I will have saved one to two times my household income.*

Be honest with yourself as your look at your answers. Are you aiming for what you want? Greatness is never achieved through small goals. Set high standards for yourself and begin the climb.

MILLENNIAL MONEY MAKEOVER PRINCIPLE OF SUCCESS: THINKING BIG MAKES YOU WIN BIG

Constructing the ideal future is no small task. Be imaginative and bold with your goals and bask in the process. The higher you aim, the bigger you will win. Push yourself and your life forward.

The Professional

At some moment (hopefully today), you will decide to change the direction of your life. When you realize that being in debt sucks, a lack of savings breeds anxiety, and that your future is purely in your hands, action is required. Deciding to turn professional is never easy, but once you taste success, you will find yourself looking back and wondering why you didn't act sooner.

As a professional you will:

- Increase your confidence
- Change the direction of your life
- Grasp the concept of the J-curve
- Work on creating good financial habits
- Develop short- and long-term goals
- Internalize sound financial judgment

As you will see in the next chapter, the second major step in the money makeover is to eliminate all of your debt quickly. There will be moments when it seems hard, but ride through the dip of the J-curve and remember that success is on the horizon. Encourage yourself with positive self-talk and reinforce your successes. When the going gets tough, remember that you have someone here who cares about your success and wants you to change the road you are on.

Welcome to the professional life.

Action Items

The money makeover is all about momentum. With inertia on your side, you can start to make positive change in your financial life. Throughout this book, you will incrementally build upon the ideas presented in this chapter. While absorbing and implementing this new skill set, remember the following steps:

1. Decide to turn professional with your money.
2. Build up confidence in yourself and your abilities.

3. Break bad habits and learn now to create new ones.

4. Set short- and long-term goals.

5. Decide to go all in on your money makeover.

Accelerate your money makeover by internalizing everything that is laid out in the following chapters; they are here to change your life.

2

··

Red to Black: How to Pay Off Credit Cards and Student Loans

Resistance is the enemy within.
—Steven Pressfield, *The War of Art*[1]

In a cartoon published by *The New Yorker*, a handsomely dressed man and a pearl-wearing woman are sitting at their chic kitchen table staring at one another before dinner. The man slowly leans over to the beautiful woman and says, "Love you, love us, and I'm comfortable with our debt level."

Debt has snuck its way into the lives of millions of Millennials. The problem, of course, is that it never wants to sneak out. Debt is like the unannounced visitor who shows up and wants to crash on your couch "just for a few days."

If you want to escape debt, there is only one way to do it, and you must to it right. If you don't, debt will outstay its welcome. Something tells me it already has.

Luckily, you only face a binary choice with debt: Keep it in your life or eliminate it. There are thousands of success stories about intelligent, motivated, and hard-working people who have taken the necessary steps to pay off thousands of dollars of debt and claim back their financial future. My goal is for you to become one of those people.

Why Debt Sucks

Debt offers a homily of hollowness. You cannot quite understand this when you are using debt; its intoxicating grip blinds you. Signing up for new credit cards is effortless. Applying for a large student loan is now pedestrian. But debt only tighens its grip when you want to eliminate it. You will find yourself wishing you could wave a magic wand and have your debt instantly forgiven. Unfortunately, that is not going to happen (how sweet would that be though?). The only way to kick debt out of your life is to focus on your future and prepare.

Debt sucks; it really does. When you start the process of paying off credit card debt or student loans, you will come up with *every* plausible scenario why you shoudn't pay the debt back as quickly as possible. *What if something happens? Is my emergency fund big enough? Does it matter if I pay it down quickly?*

That voice in your head is called "resistance," and it is the force that works against you in your money makeover. In this book, you will learn to fight resistance and defeat it. Instead of avoiding the steps to become debt free, you are going to lean in and do exactly what needs to be done. As you make progress and start to pay off small balances of debt, your resolve will become stronger. And when you get close to the point of having no debt at all, or crossing the threshold from red to black, you will become ecstatic. The moment you cross that line will be one that you remember for the rest of your life.

The reason I am so passionate about personal finance is that I get to watch thousands of people cross the debt-free finish line. My goal is to help as many people as I can cross that line. Once you do, the future is wide open. You understand that *you* have the *power* to do whatever you want in life. The momentum of that progress changes lives. I know it will change yours too.

Before we get too far, there is something that you have to do: Break up with your debt. Say goodbye to it once and for all. Delete its number. No late-night texts. No drunken calls. No Facebook stalking. It. Is. Over.

This is not going to be easy, but neither is a meaningful makeover. I know you are anxious to get started, so let's get educated on why debt likes to hang around in the first place. That will help you understand how and why you should lead a debt-free life.

Interest: The Silent Killer

Why is debt so bad? The answer lies in the fine print.

When people purchase with credit, they fail to calculate the total cost of purchase (TCP), which is often much higher than the initial sticker price. The primary driver of this difference is interest, which has a tendency to catch people off guard.

Let's examine the basics. Whether you are using credit cards, taking out a student loan, financing a new car, or buying a house, the same process is occurring. A lender (the guy with the cash) is allowing the borrower (the guy without the cash) to use the lender's money *today* based on a promise that the borrower will pay back the money in the *future*.

This means that the lender has to delay consumption or defer other investment opportunities. In exchange for using the lender's money, the lender charges an interest rate to the borrower. This interest rate is intended to compensate the lender for both the risk that the borrower might *not* repay the loan and for the lender's delayed consumption. Sounds fair, right?

Each type of debt has three major variables: The first is the size of the loan, or principal. This can vary from hundreds of dollars into the trillions. The second is the loan's maturity, or length of the loan. Loan maturity can vary significantly, with short-term loans only lasting days or months and long-term loans lasting one year or more. The third is the riskiness of the borrower. Some borrowers have excellent track records for paying back debt and others do not. As a result, the lender charges the borrower an interest rate based on the unique blend of principal, loan maturity, and riskiness. The critical point to keep in mind is that not all debt is created equal.

Some debt is high risk (a borrower who has defaulted on previous loans) for the lender, and therefore the lender charges a premium to borrow their money. When the interest for this loan kicks in, the total cost of purchase begins to increase drastically.

Take a look at the following table for varying interest rate averages on typical types of credit.[2]

Types of Credit	Average Annual Interest Rate	Happiness Calculator
Credit Cards	13%	☹
Student Loans	8%	☹
Consumer Loans	6%	☺
Mortgages	4%	☺

As you can see, the highest interest rates are often associated with credit cards, followed by student loans, consumer loans, and mortgages. Interest rates are silent killers because most borrowers tend to forget that interest rates are even there until the size of their loan has gotten out of control.

Let's look at Lisa, a graduate student, as an example. She needs a new computer for her classes and decides to purchase the latest MacBook Pro for $2,000. Because Lisa doesn't have any income, she decides to keep the small amount of cash she does have for daily expenses. So she purchases the new computer with her credit card, which has an average interest rate of 13 percent.

Once Lisa starts her semester she becomes engrossed in her schoolwork and realizes she doesn't have time for a part-time job, like she planned, to pay off her computer. The first month's credit card bill goes unpaid, then the second month, and then the third. Busy with assignments, Lisa decides to defer paying her credit card bill entirely until after the school year is over.

Instead of the MacBook Pro costing Lisa the initial purchase price of $2,000, $260 of interest accrued, now making the computer a $2,260 purchase!

Let's also assume that Lisa has to finance her two-year master's program. Once she graduates and enters the working world, life gets a little messy and she defers payment on her credit card and student loans for several years. Take a look at Lisa's computer and student loan costs now.

Lisa delays paying for her purchase immediately, and as a result interest on her purchase begins to accrue and eventually skyrockets the cost of the initial purchase. If you do not make the conscious choice to eliminate debt quickly, it can balloon out of control.

Lisa's Graduate School Expenses			
Timeline	Computer	Student Loan	Total Debt
Purchase	$2,000	$20,000	$22,000
Year 1	$2,260	$21,600	$23,860
Year 2	$2,554	$23,328	$25,882
Year 3	$2,886	$25,194	$28,080
Year 4	$3,261	$27,210	$30,471
Year 5	$3,685	$29,387	$33,072

By starting the money makeover, you will save yourself time, money, and heartache. Paying off your debt as quickly as possible is a winning strategy. You have already decided to turn professional with your money. It is time to finally get debt free, which begins with eliminating your credit card debt.

Part 1: Credit Cards

I Owe You: A Money Problem

In 2017, credit card users racked up a total of $1.021 trillion in outstanding revolving credit, the highest in US history.[3] As these numbers continue to climb, industry experts are concerned that this level of debt has infected wealth generation. Instead of young professionals purchasing productive income-producing assets and investments, which is needed to generate wealth, those with higher debt levels are using their discretionary cash to service their debt by making principal and interest payments. This impedes the start of their wealth accumulation.

In an interview with *MarketWatch*, Matt Schulz, a senior industry analyst at CreditCards.com, highlights the importance of the milestone. "This record should serve as a wake-up call to Americans to focus on their credit card debt. Even if you feel your debt is manageable right now, know that you could be one unexpected emergency away from real trouble."[4]

Americans have a debt problem, and credit card companies are willing enablers. Lenders focus on the strength of their marketing, with household names such as Amex, Capital One, Citigroup, and J.P. Morgan spending a combined $850 million on advertising alone.[5] Their strategy for customer acquisition has paid off; more than 70 percent of Americans have at least one credit card, and roughly half of all Millennials have at least three cards.[6] Nearly 83 percent of these Millennials carry a revolving credit card debt with balances ranging from $1,000 to $4,999.[7]

The revolving debt is a major problem as two thirds of Millennials have less than $1,000 in their savings accounts.[8] That means when the unexpected expense hits—the car breaks down, the pet gets sick, the computer goes on the fritz—credit card users will find themselves in a major bind. With their debt outpacing their savings, Millennials will have to borrow more to cover the cost, and the cycle of debt will continue.

The culture of debt is challenging to escape because people often rationalize the use of credit cards. People tell themselves that *they* are different from everyone else when it comes to credit cards. *They* can make the monthly payments on time. *They* understand the value of money and managing credit. But *they* usually end up in credit card debt.

In 2016, American Express made nearly $34 billion in revenue.[9] Part of that revenue comes from profits they make on people spending more than they earn. Their business model is built on the assumption that people will *not* manage their household cash flow appropriately, and for many households, the excessive use of credit cards continues to validate this assumption.

I am about to give you the secret on how to beat credit card companies, which will save you thousands of dollars in interest payments, late fees, and annual fees. This may even add years to your life (study still in progress). If you adopt this secret, you will be well on your way to becoming rich.

The secret is: *Do not play their game.*

The media does a terrific job of giving people *thousands* of reasons why they should use credit cards. In turn, I can give you *141 million* people who are in credit card debt (just in the US alone).[10] If you plan your monthly cash flow, build up savings, and do not use credit cards, life will *still* be good.

In fact, you will be well on your way to the rich life. Don't use credit cards and your life will improve drastically. I guarantee it.

By using credit cards, you are able to self-talk your way into spending more than you should. Credit cards do a remarkable job of reducing the friction of a purchase, or as economists call it, "the pain of the transaction." This reduced friction causes amnesia that causes people to keep spending, and that is the key to the credit card industry's success.

Take the following quiz and see if you fall into the trap of relying too much on credit cards for your daily spending. Give it a try by downloading a spreadsheet with blank answers at MillennialMoneyMakeover.com.

Reflection Questions	Sample Answers
Do I buy items even when I do not have enough cash to make the purchase?	*Yes, especially when I want to buy something I haven't budgeted for.*
Do I say, "I'll find a way to pay for this later?"	*I always try to find a way to defer payment because cash is scarce.*
Do I buy more expensive products with my credit card than with cash or a debit card?	*When I use my credit card, I always seem to run up charges out of nowhere.*
Do I begin my social outing with "I got this!" even when I know I do not?	*Unfortunately, yes. I get caught up in the moment too often.*
Do I pay with credit cards in a social setting because everyone else is paying that way too?	*It seems easier that way, right? But I end up paying way more than I want.*
Do I always pay my full credit card balance each month?	*No. Some months go unpaid. That seems to begin my credit card debt spiral.*
How many credit cards do I have?	*I have four!*

Take some time to think about your answers, and don't get stressed out as you answer. This is just a starting point to help you realize you don't *need* to use credit cards. Instead, you are going to learn that using cash or a debit card will significantly mitigate overspending.

....

MILLENNIAL MONEY MAKEOVER PRINCIPLE OF SUCCESS: CASH IS FOREVER KING

Cash is here to help. It beats all other forms of payment and should be kept around instead of given away. Keep this principle at the top of your financial decision tree.

....

The Balancing Act

Managing multiple credits cards is like juggling on a tightrope—and Millennials can be adrenaline junkies. However, credit cards are not to be taken lightly because once they enter your financial ecosystem, they are difficult to eliminate. You might have initially thought that you only needed one credit card, but something tells me it didn't stop there.

Your first credit card was probably used as a financial crutch to fuel your lifestyle. Then you started relying on it, and that is where things got derailed. Now you get annoyed at minimum payments, interest fees, and annual fees as they erode your already limited discretionary income. Suddenly, the rewards don't seem worth the effort, and you start shopping around for better cards with more perks. This leads to more credit card applications. Before you know it, you have two, three, or four credit cards— all with varying balances.

To avoid the balancing act altogether, the best strategy is to get rid of one credit card at a time. Pick your favorite and say goodbye to the rest. The disadvantages of having multiple credit cards include:

- Difficulty in managing payment schedules and due dates

- Paying the wrong amount per card, which leads to late fees

- Overconsumption with numerous cards, which leads to higher debt

- Opening a new card to solve another financial problem[11]

Once you decide to stop using credit cards, it is essential to examine why you signed up for multiple credit cards in the first place. There may be various influencers in your life; identify them and remove them.

Perhaps hanging out with a specific group of friends is causing you to overspend (these are your Joneses). Maybe your choice of apartments left you house rich and cash poor (perhaps you need to move). Maybe you are spending too much on travel (find local events). Whatever the reason, it is crucial to pinpoint the "why" behind signing up for multiple credit cards. Go to MillennialMoneyMakeover.com to download the following spreadsheet and fill in your own answers.

Reason	Sample Answers
First reason	*My credit cards fueled my weekend warrior lifestyle.*
Second reason	*My shopping got out of control.*
Third reason	*My rent was too high and did not leave me with enough money to go out to eat or do anything social.*

Now that you have identified *why* you have too many credit cards, it is time to have an intervention. Admit to yourself that you have a problem. I am sure it was a fun ride while it lasted, but it's time to get rid of your credit cards once and for all. No more excuses!

Eliminating credit card debt may take some realignment of priorities. You should be realistic with yourself; this is going to take some time. Now that you identified the three main reasons for why you signed up for credit cards, you need to eliminate those variables. This might mean having some tough conversations with yourself and others, but that means you are getting closer to financial freedom.

The hard part of any balancing act is the dismount. Now that you know juggling multiple credit cards is a recipe for financial disaster, it is time to cut up your cards.

The act is over.

Seven Steps to Paying Off Credit Card Debt

Debt has crept into the daily ebb and flow of American life. In 2017, the average household that carried credit card debt had a balance of $15,654.[12] The absurdity of that situation is our reality. As Millennials, we wake up in a house we don't own, put on clothes purchased with credit, and drive to work in financed cars. This presents a problem that we need to acknowledge.

Missing monthly payments, making costly impulse purchases, and spending more in general are all consumer behaviors that credit card companies count on to snare consumers. These habits lead to the cycle of credit card entanglement. It is not until the heady elixir of easy money wears off that most people start facing the reality of their predicament.

But once you are ready for the detoxification, use the following step-by-step strategy to help you pay off credit card debt fast.

Step 1. Acknowledge Your Credit Card Debt

As with most interventions, the first step toward behavioral change is an acknowledgment that a problem exists. Your debt comes from a pattern of overspending or poor financial planning. So far, you reviewed the three main reasons why you opened your credit cards in the first place; make sure that you are eliminating these variables from your life.

Next, construct a full inventory of your purchasing habits and analyze your consumption. Take a look at your last three months of credit card statements and print them out (yes, you need to do this). Use a highlighter and mark each purchase that you didn't *need*. After you are done highlighting those purchases, total all of your highlighted purchases and write down that total. Something tells me it is higher than you initially thought.

Once you know this number, go through the following self-assessment:

- What purchases led you to use your credit cards?
- Did you use your credit cards in specific situations?
- Did you use your credit card impulsively or because of poor planning?
- Did monthly subscriptions get the better of you?

Now that you have examined your spending you can take refuge in the fact that this was *past* spending. Your past does not define today. You have made the critical decision to acknowledge the problem and slash your credit card debt.

Step 2. List Your Credit Card Debts in Ascending Order

Pull out all of your credit cards and lay them on a table. Sort them by balance, starting with the smallest balance first and working your way toward the largest balance. This process helps you visualize how many cards you are using and gives you a keen sense of what you are up against.

Once you have all of your credit cards laid out in the correct order, fill in the following chart, which will provide a visual of what debts to attack first. You can download a blank spreadsheet at MillennialMoneyMakeover.com. Remember to list your credit cards in ascending order based on the card's total balance.

Credit Card	Monthly Minimum	Total Balance	Reason You Opened
American Express	$35	$550	Flight home
Discover	$25	$700	Bachelorette party
Capital One	$35	$1,500	Work clothes
Bank of America	$20	$2,000	Going out
Chase	$25	$2,500	Apartment furniture

The smallest balance on your list is what you are going to attack and eliminate first. Write down the amount and post it in a prominent place. Look at it repeatedly. That number is your first target.

Step 3. Create a Flash Budget

Now that you know what credit card to pay off first, you can start building what I like to call a flash budget. Start by analyzing your monthly income and expenses, and list all sources of income. Once that is complete, create another list of your fixed expenses, or expenses that are not going to change from month to month (rent, car payments, insurance, and so on). Once you have your fixed costs summarized, list your monthly variable costs. Variable costs are costs that fluctuate based on the level of activity (going out to eat, drinks, clothes, and so on).

Finally, subtract expenses from your income. This reveals your margin of error. Let's say you have $1,000 left over after you subtract expenses from your income. That $1,000 should go toward paying off the lowest credit card balance.

Reworking your budget to meet your current debt repayment needs might take some adjusting. For now, you can focus on either increasing your earnings or cutting your costs. Once you have created your flash budget, it will be important to develop a much more refined budget for long-term success (see Chapter 3).

Your budget will serve as an unbiased performance evaluator, which will hold you accountable for every purchase.

Step 4. Snowball Your Success

One of the most critical aspects of getting rid of debt is a behavioral modification. The positive psychological impact of gaining incremental success by paying down your smallest debt first is crucial.

Conventional wisdom will tell you otherwise. This view advocates paying off your debts beginning with the highest interest rates first. Talking heads and television personalities love preaching this drivel as gospel. They argue that paying off the credit cards with the highest APR reduces the overall cost of credit cards in the long term. From a purely economic perspective, they are correct.

But as we know, personal finance is about much more than numbers. Although this approach makes the most economic sense, paying off debt quickly doesn't happen in a vacuum. Debt repayment is more about behavioral change than pure economics. Researchers at Northwestern University's Kellogg School of Management found that consumers who tackle small balances first are more likely to eliminate their overall debt.[13] By paying off your smallest balances first, you create momentum. This leads to higher confidence to tackle the larger balances in your debt portfolio. Plus, watching the lines on your repayment spreadsheet disappear is magical.

Step 5. Pay With Cash

Once you begin the positive cycle of paying off your smaller credit card balances, you should focus next on how you are going to fund your day-to-day purchases. Because you fell prey to the frictionless form of credit card payment, you should start using cash for daily transactions.

There are many benefits to paying with cash. First, cash gives you a tangible and visible pulse on how well you are sticking to your budget. Second, making payments with cash will force you to pause and contemplate the magnitude of each purchase.

It may seem counterintuitive, but increasing the pain of the transaction is better for your financial health. Paying for expenses with cash gives you a clear view of your monthly cash flow. This small change will stem your spending.

Step 6. Celebrate Your Wins

As with any significant accomplishment, it is important to acknowledge your small victories along the way. Each time you pay off a credit card balance, celebrate your success (using the cash from Step 5) and reward yourself. Go to the movies, go out to dinner, go to a sporting event, or go to an art class. As you approach your final payment, the rewards will become less frequent because your balances increase. But realize the ultimate prize of becoming debt free is just on the horizon.

Step 7. Share Your Success

As you develop new spending habits, it will become important to reflect on your experience. The process of sharing your success with family and friends allows you to prime yourself for successful habits and cultivate a sense of accomplishment. In addition, reflecting and internalizing your daily financial wins improves your success rate. This routine helps you ensnare the credit card spending you are fighting to contain and may unknowingly help someone else along the way.

....

Money Makeover Pro Tip:
How to Spend Less When You Go Out

When you go out with friends, follow these steps to control your spending: 1) Set a spending limit for the night; 2) get out cash before you leave; 3) leave your credit card at home; and 4) stick to your budget.

....

How to Talk with Credit Card Representatives

What you learn in this section will pay for this book. In fact, you are going to reap a huge return on your investment. The only caveat is that you will need to pick up the phone and do a little work.

Most credit cards come with an annual fee and high penalties for missing payments. These fees are a terrific way for credit card companies to increase their annual revenue in an already lucrative business. Often, card companies automatically lump the annual fee onto your bill without your knowledge. Stop for a moment and look at your credit card statements. Do you see the fee?

Once you find the fee, it's time to give your credit card company a call. I want you to chat with a credit card representative and get your annual fee waived. I know you think this will be awkward. But the reality is that you have the upper hand. Credit card companies place a tremendous value on keeping customers because the average American household pays hundreds of dollars in interest each year. Credit card companies are inclined to credit back an annual fee or interest charge because they think it will be a one-time event. Little do they know that you are going to eliminate your credit card debt altogether and be done with them for good!

Remember: If you get freaked out during this process, all you have to do is hang up. If things don't work out with the first call, you can always call back. Keep calling until the fee is reversed. Use the following script to help guide you through the call.

Me: Hello, I was calling to discuss the annual fee for my [fill in the blank] credit card.

Rep: Good day, Mr. Richardson. Let me see here. Yes, your annual fee is $20.

Me: Thank you for taking the time to look that up. Can you please go ahead and credit that back to my card? I don't want to pay an annual fee for my credit card.

Rep: Oh, I am sorry, Mr. Richardson. I am not able to do that in our system.

Me: Look, I just started the Millennial Money Makeover challenge, and I am consciously working on paying off my credit card balances as quickly as possible. The charge you are looking at occurred in a hectic month. Can you please credit it back into my account?

Rep: Let me take a look at your account. Can you hold?

Me: Yes, of course.

Rep: Mr. Richardson, I have great news. I spoke with my manager and we have credited back your annual fee. You should see it come through in the next couple of days.

Me: Thank you very much.

Rep: Is there anything else that I can help you with today?

Me: That is all. Have a great day!

I know what you are thinking: This can't possibly work. However, if you are forcefully polite, you can get your annual fees waived. It simply involves taking a few minutes to call your credit card company and begin the conversation. Once you have the call, it only takes two to three business days for the charges to be credited back to your account. That's money back in your pocket!

But wait, we aren't done yet. As we learned earlier, the power of reaching milestones toward a larger goal can spur success. Keep that in mind here, too. After you see your annual fee credited back to your account, it will be time to get back on the phone. If you had an interest payment in the past twelve months, get the most recent interest charge credited back to your account too (simply substitute "interest fee" for "annual fee" in the script provided). Keep the momentum going and build your confidence.

Remember: Credit card debt is something that you control. Financial experts such as Ramit Sethi, author of *I Will Teach You to Be Rich,* have evangelized this hack of taking control of your credit card interest payments and annual fees because it really does work. It puts money back into your pocket while simultaneously boosting your confidence. Accepting this responsibility is key to your money makeover.

How to Dominate Credit Cards

In today's economy, it seems like having a credit card is a must. Truthfully, there are only a couple of situations in which you need a credit card. For those rare occasions, you might as well have a good one.

There is a right way to use credit cards and it is not hard, if you can avoid the temptation of overspending. I advise having only one emergency credit card. But once you have built up your emergency saving fund (see Chapter 4), the sole purpose of this credit card should be for vendors who do not accept cash.

Until then, here are five ways to dominate credit cards:

Get a Credit Card With Awesome Rewards

If you must have a credit card, make sure you have one that works to your advantage. There are countless options to choose from, so do your homework and get one with a low APR and a high reward-to-expense ratio.

Credit card companies offer a variety of different rewards as incentive to use their cards, including cash back and travel points. I recommend the travel rewards because they can offer the highest return. Although 1 to 5 percent cash back sounds like a great deal upfront, the real winnings come when you can purchase flights or book free hotel rooms.

Always Pay Your Full Balance

This sounds like a no-brainer, but this is the exact reason why credit card companies exist. Credit cards companies thrive off of human fallibility, that is, late payments and financed purchases.

If you are opening up a rewards credit card, set aside some cash for the credit card *before* you open it. Think of this as a hedge against your future cash flows. Every time you make a credit card purchase, transfer money from your checking account to the credit card. In other words, pay for the purchase every time you use your credit card! This prevents forgotten purchases and missed due dates, and ensures the integrity of the pain of the transaction.

Monitor Your Credit Utilization

As you start to conquer your credit cards, it is important to eliminate them from your life one by one. That means closing each account as you pay off the card. The ill informed will advise against this because it can negatively affect your credit utilization in the short term. Let's dive into why.

Your credit score is comprised of several components, one of which is your credit utilization ratio. This ratio influences part of your FICO credit score, which analyzes your credit worthiness to lenders. In short, your credit utilization is the amount of credit that you use, calculated as a percent of your total credit limit. For example:

- Card A has a $1,000 balance with a $5,000 limit.
- Card B has a $4,000 balance with a $10,000 limit.
- Card C has a $0 balance with a $5,000 limit.

In this scenario, your credit utilization is the total $5,000 of credit card balances divided by the $20,000 of available credit card limits, or 25 percent. If you close Credit Card C because you just recently paid it off, then your credit card utilization jumps to 33 percent ($5,000/$15,000). This higher credit utilization is viewed as a negative by lenders because you are using a considerable portion of your credit available, which increases your risk of default. The reality is that this does not matter in the long run.

As you eliminate debt from your life and close credit cards, your credit utilization will decrease. But once you are to the point of using one credit card, all you have to do is call the credit card company (yes, again) and ask them to raise the credit limit on that one card. This will increase your credit utilization score.

Damaging your credit score can increase the cost of big-ticket items because lenders will demand a higher interest rate when you borrow money. If you are about to buy a house or take out a student loan, then it will be important to consider your credit utilization. You can optimize control over your debt by making automatic payments to the credit card you choose to keep (see Chapter 6).

Negotiate a Lower APR

Credit card companies are basically legalized loan sharks. If you don't make your payments, they come a-knocking. And when they do, they can demand exorbitant interest on unpaid portions of your debt.

An annual percentage rate (APR) is the annual rate that is charged for borrowing money and is expressed as a single percentage, which represents the actual yearly cost of funds over the term of a loan. This includes any fees or additional costs associated with the transaction.[14] The higher the APR, the worst it is for you, the borrower.

Call your credit card company and ask them to decrease your credit card's APR. Yes, you can do this. For some reason, most people don't and end up paying far more than they need to. This costs them big.

Keep a Lockbox

When you are done using credit cards and setting up your automatic deposits, it will be important to keep all of your credit cards stored in a central location. This is your lockbox, which can be a physical or virtual location.

Keep your lock box well accounted for. With the rampant degree of credit card fraud and identity theft taking place every day, you do not want your information getting into the wrong hands. Storing your cards in one location will make the maintenance hassle-free.

Let me be clear: I recommend having *one* credit card. Use resources such as NerdWallet.com, CreditCards.com, and ConsumerReports.org to shop for the best credit cards available. These sites do a fantastic job with their credit card comparison tools, which can help you find the best credit card for you. When you find the *one* credit card you want to use, stick with it and don't open any others.

Although I advocate having no credit card debt, as technology improves and our economy moves toward more digital payments, some businesses will not accept cash. Only use your credit card in these rare circumstances.

Keep Your Momentum

Once the momentum of paying off your credit cards begins to build, you will get hooked on the idea of becoming debt free. Watching your debt number approach zero will become addicting. You will slowly begin to taste the autonomy produced by living debt free.

As marathon runners say, the race truly begins at mile 20. When you get closer to crossing from red to black, dig in and pick up your speed. Once you eliminate credit card debt from your diet, it is time to keep the momentum going and move on to any other debt you may have, such as student loans or consumer debt.

Getting to zero is worth every second of the struggle. Ride the wave of momentum in your makeover money.

Part 2: Student Loans

Student Loans: An Educated Beast

In a satirical article by *The Onion* entitled "Teary-Eyed Student Loan Officers Proudly Watch As $200,000 Asset Graduates from College," loan officers from Sallie Mae are described as being hyper emotional at an undergraduate graduation ceremony from Emory University in Atlanta,

Georgia. Loan officers were quoted as saying, "It's been absolutely amazing to watch our revenue stream grow right before our eyes." The officer's optimism was captured even further when describing their hope that "one day they may be able to see their source of profit go to law school."[15] The article captures the painful realities that engulf today's student loan crisis.

Student loans have become a hot topic for Millennials because most Millennials have either felt the weight of student loans or know of someone who is struggling to pay them off. Chronic student loans are a financial epidemic.

As of the writing of this book, the nation's student loan balance has risen to $1.3 trillion, up from $447 billion only ten years ago.[16] Ballooning student debt is getting out of control as people continue to invest in the belief that a four-year college is automatically the right path for everyone. The average student loan debt is at a historic high and has increased at a pace of 6 percent faster than inflation over the past decade.[17] As the cost of education continues to soar, so too do correlated student loans.

Education is a gift that has traditionally stamped the ticket to success. But the socioeconomic propulsion it once provided seems to be fading. The American educational success sequence—studying hard, making good grades, attending a top college, and landing a great job—is beginning to crumble. The great jobs promised in the halls of higher education are starting to disappear. This is due to a fundamental misalignment between our current education system and the rapidly evolving job market.

Don't get me wrong; student loans still provide a tremendous benefit to those who need to finance their education. Sometimes there is simply no choice. Student loans offer an avenue for determined students who want immediate access to the very best education. What we will address in this section is the spillover effect of rising loans. Although formal education can offer tremendous value, student loans often leave borrowers with years of nagging debt, stifling the dream they once set out to achieve.

My job is to help you reach those dreams and passions as fast as possible. By paying off your student loans, you will expedite your path to financial success.

The Story of Gradible

As you just read, student loan repayments have ballooned into an everyday problem for millions of Millennials. For Gradible cofounder Pete Wylie, the difficulty of helping people pay off their student loans has turned into a daily passion. In the summer of 2012, Wylie, along with cofounders Lee Smallwood and Grant Biles, brainstormed the idea behind their startup Gradible, a business dedicated to helping young professionals pay off their student loans.

After the initial concept was born, Gradible gained entry into the prestigious New York City–based seed-stage accelerator AngelPad. Founded by former Googler Thomas Korte, AngelPad is a growth lab for early-stage high-tech startups. This kind of workplace was precisely what Gradible needed to formulate the best way to help US graduates pay off their student loans.

Initially, Gradible helped recent graduates with student loan debt match up with employers who needed freelance work. The concept was that once the work was complete, employers would make payments directly to the student's outstanding debt. Grabile users loved this approach, and 87 percent of users preferred having their student loans reduced directly instead of being paid in cash. While working on this idea, it became apparent to the Gradible team that there was a massive opportunity to educate those who had student loans about the programs available to help pay off their debt. Gradible quickly pivoted to this new, and later successful, strategy.

In the fall of 2016, Gradible was acquired for an undisclosed amount by CommonBond, a leading financial technology company in the higher education space.[18] After the acquisition, Wylie joined the CommonBond team as the vice president of finance and continues to work with students to alleviate their student loan debt.

Interested to hear about what insights and suggestions Wylie would give to prospective students, I asked what recommendations he could provide. Wylie was adamant about several things he learned during his time at Gradible. In particular, he suggests considering the following three items before signing a large student loan:

1. *Consider cost of attendance.* Most people are blinded by prestigious names and acceptance letters. Sit down and honestly analyze how expensive the total cost of attendance will be and weigh that against your outcomes for employment.

2. *Make sure you graduate.* When you look at the numbers, there is a significant correlation between graduation rates and difficulty in student loans repayment. Make sure you graduate to reap the rewards of your credentials.

3. *Understand that majors matter.* Although you shouldn't always think about a college major in purely economic terms, you would be wise to factor it into your decision. Instead of majoring in philosophy

alone, why not double major in philosophy and economics? Varied majors and diversification of knowledge will help you gain employment and solve real-world problems after graduation.

Wylie also wants people to consider all of their options and use their surrounding resourses. If you already have student loan debt, consider using apps, websites, and businesses dedicated to helping you with your loan. Use all the tools at your disposal and be resourceful. The Gradibles of the world are waiting to help you.

....

Money Makeover Pro Tip:
Use Your Resources for Reducing Student Loans
Check out companies like Earnest, CommonBond, SoFi, and LendingClub to help you escape student loans.

....

Three Things No One Wants to Hear

The evidence is clear; you owe it to yourself to pay off your student loans as fast as possible. The fallacy that most people talk themselves into is that long-term debt equals long-term payments. This is false. For most student loans, interest starts to accrue right after graduation; for others, it starts when they are still in school. When this occurs, a $30,000 loan can quickly morph into $35,000. And then $40,000. And then $45,000.

This can happen within a matter of a few years, thereby increasing your total cost of education. With the average 2017 college graduate carrying a student loan debt of $37,172, interest can get out of hand quickly. To aggressively pay off your student loans, you might have to make some changes to your lifestyle. Here are three hard suggestions to hear if you have student loans.

1. Move in With Your Parents

I know you hate hearing this, but living with your parents will profoundly reduce your cash outflow. During my coaching, I found that there is serious resistance to moving back in with parents. Get over it, because your highest fixed cost after graduation will be rent. Do not pay it if you do not have to.

How will you even ask your parents?

I suggest sitting down with them, or at least the nice one, and explain that you are completing your money makeover and trying to pay off your student loans fast. The catch is that you want to move back into your old room.

If you cannot live with your parents, try living with relatives or someone else willing to lend a helping hand. Everyone understands that student loans are onerous. If you are working hard, people are usually willing to help.

2. Sell Your Nice Car

If you are driving around in a new car and you have student loans, sell the car and use the cash to pay down the loan. Technically this goes for anything of value that you own.

In all honesty, this is a no-brainer. The reason this can seem difficult is that it forces you to realize there is a major gap between where you *are* and where you *want* to be. The economic fallacy you have in your head and the reality of your current financial state do not align. Not to worry; they will soon.

3. Establish a Buddy System

Humans are social creatures. If you are looking to combat the pain of student loans, chances are one of your friends is struggling with the same predicament. You both won't have much money to spend when you are putting all of your extra cash toward paying off your student loans, so lean into that commonality with a friend.

Instead of participating in expensive activities, scour for free or cheap stuff together. Join a book club (start a *Millennial Money Makeover* book club). Go on runs. Paint. Write. Study. Exercise.

Paying Off Student Loans the SMART Way

Student loans are the red-headed stepchild of credit cards. They are often much more annoying and nobody wants to deal with them, until now.

Before we dive into paying off student loans, let me make something very clear: If you still have credit card debt, go back to Part 1 of this chapter and attack your credit cards first. Once those are eliminated, then you can start chipping away at your student loans. If you don't have credit card debt or have already paid it off, congratulations! Now it's time to move on to eliminating your student loans.

As a highly educated individual with a bachelor's, master's, doctorate, or whatever degree you possess, you should be SMART about paying back your student loans. By following the steps listed below, you will be able to pay off your student loans insanely fast.

Small Balances First

Student loans can be daunting to pay off because their sheer size is overwhelming. Acting like your student loans do not exist is a practice of self-denial. Self-preservation calls for you to address the problem.

By not paying off student loans quickly, the overall cost of the loans can dramatically increase over time as interest accumulates. This means paying off a ballooning student loan can take more of your hard-earned money out of your pocket.

You have to optimize your behavior when it comes to paying off your loans. Harness the power of behavioral modification based on the research from Northwestern University's Kellogg School of Management, which recommends you focus on paying the smallest loan first. This method increases your chance of overall success.[19] Ignore your larger loans for now and keep them at bay while you focus on eliminating your smallest loan. This will give you the momentum you need to go from red to black.

Fill in the following chart with all of your student loans in ascending order (the smallest balance first). You can download a blank version at MillennialMoneyMakeover.com.

Student Loan Lender	Balance
1. Citizens Bank	$3,000
2. Wells Fargo	$8,000
3. Discover	$10,000
4. Sallie Mae	$17,000

Pay More than the Minimum

Now that you zeroed in on your smallest loan, gather all of your resources to pay the monthly minimum. Look underneath the couch for change, sell your extra clothes, or forgo a night out with friends.

Now that you are focused on eliminating your smallest loan first, what do you do about your other loans? Because most of your cash flow is concentrated on paying off your smallest loan, you still can't lose sight of your other larger loans (if you have any). For those loans, keep paying the monthly minimum to make sure they don't balloon out of control. By paying the monthly minimum, you can effectively keep them in check.

Always Find More Money

It is time to unleash your inner entrepreneur. You need to find a way to do two things in your life: cut expenses and increase your income. Having exhausted the former, you should start focusing on how to increase your income. This is where your entrepreneurial spirit comes in. There are countless ways to earn extra money in today's shared economy, and with your intelligence and education, you will be able to find something immediately. Go to MillennialMoneyMakeover.com for ideas on how to make some extra money.

Take the time to develop a strategy and think about how you are going to pull in some extra dough. Once you start earning this extra money, throw it at your student loans and watch them melt away.

Reward Yourself

Celebrating your wins is a vital part of creating new habits. Each time you achieve a major milestone in your student loan payments, you need to reward yourself. Yes, you have my permission to splurge a little bit. When it comes to paying off your student loans, you will forgo many things that you would otherwise be spending your money on, such as clothes, vacations, or nights out.

Develop a ritual when you pay off a student loan. Whether that is having friends over for dinner, dining at your favorite restaurant, or popping a bottle of champagne, the more cadenced you make the reward, the better.

Timeline From Red To Black

This entire chapter is dedicated to the progress of going from red to black. By definition, you are in the red because you have student loan debt. Now that you have all of your student loans listed out, you should have a clear view of your minimum monthly payments. Build a flash budget by analyzing your income and expenses over the next several months (similar to what you put together in Part 1 of this chapter). Decide how much you can put toward your student loans. If you have already paid off your credit card debt, try putting the same amount each month toward your student loans and keep the ball rolling.

Once you have calculated how much you can put toward your monthly payments, it will be time to determine how long it will take for you to repay your student loans. Will it be three months, twelve months, or twenty-four months? After you have your date, mark it on your calendar. This is your blackout date—the day you cross from red to black.

While paying off your student loans the SMART way, it is important to embrace the process. After graduation, many people sulk about their student loans. Once they begin working full time, their student loan payments seems like an anchor weighing them down. It is important to remain grateful and positive about all that you learned while in school. Realize that paying off your student loans quickly is a temporary discomfort for a lifetime of knowledge.

Because you are taking the time to consciously decide to eliminate your student loans (not waiting five, ten, or fifteen years) you are adopting the makeover attitude. This attitude will launch you from red to black. The makeover journey is not solely about the money; it's about attitude. Adopt the money makeover mindset and success will quickly follow.

Three Alternatives to Higher Education

Highly motivated people often get sucked into the concept that they need to attend a prestigious and expensive school to make lots of money or find their calling. In this section, I present the case for why that is a flawed assumption.

If you want to be a doctor, you need to attend medical school. If you're going to be a dentist, then go to dental school. But some other professions might not require the conventional education plan. I urge you to consider the actual value of an advanced degree based on your career choice. The following three alternative plans can help you avoid ensnaring yourself in unnecessary long-term debt.

1. The altMBA Experience

Our educational system is broken.

Thought leaders around the country are trying to figure out ways to reduce the financial burden of our traditional educational system—a system that hampers students' post-graduation aspirations due to their massive student loans and relatively low skill set. The call for change is getting louder.

Seth Godin, bestselling author and entrepreneur, has set out on a course to correct higher education, specifically in business. That is why he started the altMBA, a new wave of disruption in the education space and one that can potentially serve as a model for the future. This one-month program gives working professionals a streamlined and immersive experience with one hundred like-minded peers.

There are no textbooks. There are no lectures. There are no $40,000 tuition payments.

The application process is rigorous, as is the experience. Students receive coaching sessions, participate in team discussions, receive a curated reading list, and they ship thirteen projects in one month. Students receive continuous assignments of "doing" throughout the program and, at the end, have something to show for their experience: a portfolio of completed projects that is instrumental in landing graduates new jobs or furthering their current careers.

And the cost according to Godin is, "A lot. $3,000. Not $2,950 or some clever amount. And it's not just the money, it's the time you'll be spending as well."[20]

Because "doing" is core to the curriculum, students complete a variety of real-world projects that give them the experience needed for post graduation success. Godin believes that students are far more capable than they know, and he pushes them toward greatness. Godin created this new program in 2012 to challenge the status quo, and things seem to be working. The program has produced more than 1,500 graduates, many from companies you may have heard of: Google, Nike, Microsoft, Johnson & Johnson, and Fidelity Investments.

2. The Dirty Experience

Mike Rowe bites goat balls.

As the host of his hit television show *Dirty Jobs,* Rowe did a lot of things he never imaged. During its eight seasons and nine-year reign on the Discovery Channel, Rowe met hundreds of skilled labors and craftsmen from all across the United States. While on the road, Rowe noticed a curious trend. At a time when the economy was tanking, people kept telling him about a shortage of skilled labor. Mike bit at the opportunity (pun intended) and in 2008 set up the mikeroweWORKS Foundation, which brings to light a discussion about "the country's dysfunctional relationship with work, highlighting the widening skills gap, and challenging the persistent belief that a four-year degree is automatically the best path for the most people."[21]

Rowe argues that there is a massive *shortage* of highly skilled labor in the market but high *demand* for these types of workers. He advocates trade school and community college as a means to jumpstart your career and to become a master of a trade. Through his foundation, Rowe has given out more than $3 million in education for trade schools around the United States.[22]

The path to success is not a one-size-fits-all model. The rich use this to their advantage and look for opportunities in unsuspecting places. In fact, they look to work and invest in areas where the competition is low and the returns are high. Rowe is highlighting a major opportunity here.

Whether it is mastering a new trade or craft, look for a new sweet spot. There are thousands of opportunities in our current economy; it is up to you to find yours.

3. The Self-Taught Experience

With one email, his life was changed forever. It wasn't an eloquent essay, but a short and concise statement of fact, sprinkled with some old-fashioned ruckus making.

In July of 2008, Josh Kaufman, a financial analyst at the time, launched himself into Internet lore when his website, PersonalMBA.com, went from a hundred readers per month to thousands of readers from all over the globe.[23] This spike in traffic happened literally overnight.

Kaufman recounts the day he sent an email to author and entrepreneur Seth Godin informing Godin of his website dedicated to business self-education. Kaufman was trying to avoid the high cost of graduate business school and adopted the mindset that a self-taught curriculum might be the better, and less expensive, solution. So he did what any good Millennial does: He started a blog. Kaufman began reading, writing, and sharing his newly developed curriculum, mostly as a means to keep himself accountable.

One day, Kaufman was reading Seth Godin's daily blog post and noticed that Godin was interested in exactly what Kaufman was working on—a website that would act as a resource for anyone interested in learning more about business. Kaufman scrambled to find Godin's email, and then Kaufman mustered up the courage to send a brief and informative email to Godin about his new business blog.

Within minutes, Godin sent out the link to Kaufman's website to his millions of readers. Kaufman's life was changed forever. PersonalMBA.com went from relative obscurity to Internet sensation. The real-world business education Kaufman was looking for came straight at him, and he seized the moment.

With the newfound traffic, Kaufman went on to secure a book deal and write *The Personal MBA: Master the Art of Business,* which later went on to become an international bestseller. Kaufman managed to avoid the high cost of graduate student loans altogether. His tuition was paid through time, energy, and hard work. *The Personal MBA* still retains an avid following and remains an excellent resource for anyone aiming to master business.

As you can see from these stories, education comes in many forms. There are countless ways to avoid the high cost of formal education. If you have already completed your advanced degree, or are currently enrolled, the lessons from Seth Godin, Mike Rowe, and Josh Kaufman apply to any point in your life.

Take this moment to reboot your thoughts about education. Learning doesn't stop after class is over. Life will present you with countless moments of self-improvement. Make your mind clearer and sharper by pursuing your education, even after class ends.

MILLENNIAL MONEY MAKEOVER PRINCIPLE OF SUCCESS: EDUCATION IS CONTINUOUS

Learning is a fixed part of life. Whether you are researching a new investment approach, consuming a new book, or listening to a podcast, self-improvement offers one of the highest returns on investment.

Publicly Declare Your Intent

Now that you have all of this knowledge on how to pay off your debt, it is time to make your commitment of being debt free public. By announcing your intention to the world, you make yourself socially accountable. That proclamation can be incredibly powerful. The pressure to perform, and to avoid social embarrassment, will drive you toward success.

I want you to declare your money makeover publicly, now.

For all of you extroverts, tell the social group that will hold you the most accountable that you have entered the Millennial Money Makeover. For you introverts, I want you to take out a sticky note and write, "Millennial Money Makeover: Challenge Accepted." Place this note on your mirror, phone, journal, or refrigerator. Just make sure it is *prominently* displayed.

A great way to find the support you need is to get social. Find the Facebook, Reddit, Instagram, or Twitter community dedicated to the love of debt-free living, building up savings, and investing. Be strategic and join those communities as soon as possible. They will provide affirmation that you are on the right track.

Once you declare your intent, a social transformation begins. Getting family and friends involved with your money makeover might spark some unexpected and exciting conversations. Perhaps some of your loved ones will confess they too have been thinking about getting their finances in order.

If you can find someone to team up with, do it! The buddy system produces tremendous benefits, so try and find a friend, girlfriend, boyfriend, or family member who understands what you are trying to accomplish. Ask them to support you along the journey and hold you accountable.

There are thousands of people in the Millennial Money Makeover community. All you have to do is start participating in the conversation. Your curious quotient will begin to increase the more you learn about money. This is when you need to put your pursuit in overdrive.

Developing Your Debt-Free Timeline

After being around highly successful venture capitalists, bankers, and business leaders, I have learned a consistent maxim: Planning is directly correlated with long-term success. Those who take the time to contemplate what they want to achieve and give themselves the necessary time and resources are always more prepared in the long run. In the world of personal finance, mapping out your strategic path to wealth can be the difference between success and failure.

Selecting goals and developing a path to reach your goals forces you to visualize the future and anticipate roadblocks. It is essential to plot out *exactly* how you are going to achieve your goal of becoming debt free.

When you are putting pen to paper, remember that many people overestimate what they can do in one day but underestimate what they can accomplish in one year. Give yourself at least twelve months to become debt free. Some people will finish their transformation faster, others slower. What matters is that you assign yourself clear objectives and timelines.

The clock has already started; your money makeover is already underway.

> *"A goal without a plan is just a wish."*
> —Antoine de Saint-Exupery[24]

The good news is that you have already taken the first step: interest in this book. This book spoke to you on some fundamental level. That little voice inside your head told you to pick it up and start your makeover. Whether you are looking to pay off credit card debt, consumer loans, or student loans, give yourself a reasonable timeline but stay aggressive.

The sooner you are debt free, the closer you are to crossing from red into black.

Action Items

Hopefully, this chapter has taught you at least one important piece of information: Debt sucks. To eventually cross from red to black you need to eliminate all forms of debt from your life. Get rid of it once and for all. Fight the resistance to pay off debt slowly and be super aggressive. You will thank yourself later.

When you are paying off debt, remember to follow these steps and get your debt snowball rolling today.

1. Commit to getting rid of all your debts.
2. Pay off your credit card debt starting with the smallest balance first.
3. Eliminate your student loans and other consumer debts.

4. Share your success with the world and keep your momentum going.

5. Stick to your debt-free timeline and action plan.

If you have credit cards or student loans, eliminating these from your life will lift a weight off of your shoulders. No longer will you remain encumbered to their principal and interest payments. Instead, you will be able to use your money to start building up a savings cushion and begin investing. In the next chapter, you will learn how to construct a budget that will set you up for long-term success. Building a passion budget will change your life and provide you with a blueprint, paving the way to a rich life.

Becoming debt free and crossing from red into black is a liberating experience. As you get closer to that line, I encourage you to share your success with as many people as possible. You will be an inspiration to others slogging their way through debt.

Once you cross the debt-free line, you will remember your life in two parts: before being in debt and after. After is better.

3

PASSION BUDGETING: HOW IT WILL CHANGE YOUR LIFE FOR THE BETTER

The bestway to predict your future is to create it.
—Peter Drucker[1]

In a cartoon published by *The New Yorker,* two sharks are swimming together in the open ocean. One shark looks over at the other and says, "I start every diet with the best intentions, but it goes to hell as soon as I sense blood in the water."

Before you try to skip the chapter on budgeting, stop! This is not going to be about cutting out all of the things you love in life. Instead, you are going to learn how to create a budget that keeps everything important to you and eliminates everything else. Yes, you will learn how to be more economical with your purchases and leverage your existing expenses. Yes, you will analyze your incomes and learn how to increase and optimize their power. Yes, you will learn rules of the road and set achievable goals. Yes, you will learn passion budgeting.

Rich people don't focus on the small things; they spend their energy applying the appropriate amount of pressure to

MILLENNIAL MONEY MAKEOVER

the right areas in order to produce maximum results. Rich people do not get distracted.

Who Actually Budgets?

Although the budgeting process may appear dull, embracing the core concepts is the key to getting where you want to go. It can even be cathartic. Before your money makeover, you might have thought that you didn't need to create a budget. After all, you probably have a good understanding of the underlying equation: income minus expenses.

The physical process of sitting down and writing out all of your cash inflows and outflows can be an incredibly powerful and motivating event. That is why the wealthy use it to their advantage. In a recent study, more than 54 percent of affluent investors create a budget and more than 84 percent stick to it.[2] This type of proactive planning is used to build and maintain their rich lives.

Some of your favorite companies, such as Apple, Nike, Amazon, Target, and Coca-Cola, also develop operating budgets every year. During the budgeting process, key stakeholders determine their goals, strategies, and objectives for the coming year. Then they prioritize what expenses will help them reach their goals. Budeting is an iterative process, but highly successful companies understand it, and so should you. Here are some examples of entities that budget:

- Startups
- Hospitals
- Universities
- Large corporations
- Not-for-profits

Chances are that you have been to one of these places recently, maybe a hospital. I bet the hospital's budgeting process never crossed your mind. I'm guessing you didn't stop to think, "This hospital's operating budget must be huge. Look at all the doctors, nurses, and administrators required to keep this place running."

Instead, you probably walked in, sat down in the waiting room, filled out an ungodly amount of paperwork, and then saw your doctor. But behind the scenes, the engines were humming.

To keep the business of "you" operating like a well-oiled machine, you must have a robust understanding of your cash flow. Gone are the days when you never analyze your income. Gone are the days when you don't think about how much money you spend. Gone are the days of claiming ignorance. Though you don't have to memorize every expense or transaction in your life, you do have to have a holistic understanding of them.

A money makeover is completed in incremental steps. It takes time, patience, and practice, but it produces disproportionate results. Those who take the time to budget win big. That is exactly what you will do here.

Think Big, Win Big

The human brain is an incredibly powerful tool. Our brain allows us to do extraordinary things like remember the past and predict the future. Our capacity for forethought, contemplating the future, and premeditation are uniquely human. Success, it turns out, is deeply rooted in our ability to see the future.

In psychology, there are countless pages of research dedicated to the study of goals and goal-setting. This information provides researchers a glimpse into how humans create the future. In this research, a concept known as goal self-perpetuation explains the reason for mounting success. The idea is that if people set real reachable goals, they will further their success by producing an environment in which winning is attainable. That is precisely what budgeting achieves: the process of setting up small wins that eventually compound into success.

Budgeting also sets up financial bumpers to keep you in line. For some reason, people tend to cringe at the idea of these boundaries. The highly personal nature of budgets produces this visceral reaction. If you boil a budget down to its component parts, a budget encompasses all of the underlying benchmarks by which society judges people: how much money you make, how much you spend, and how much wealth you have accumulated.

You were not taught how to budget properly in school. As a result, you have fear about how to set up a budget correctly. Getting a grip on your finances and budget is the fastest way to gain confidence and correct the areas of uneasiness: income, spending, and savings. The good news is that I am going to teach you how to create a budget. You will be able to use this method for the rest of your life and tailor your budget to meet both your short-term and long-term goals. Once you grasp this concept, you will be able to dominate your finances.

The beautiful thing about budgets is that they give you total autonomy. The independence and freedom to dictate your future are remarkably empowering. You hold your future in your hands. Budgeting for today, this month, or this year will set you up to win big in the future.

The Pareto Principle

Efficiency is something that we all crave. Every business, nonprofit, and household wants to yield more output with fewer inputs. This impulse to operate efficiently is rooted in our desire to spend more time doing the things we love. In budgeting, this can be accomplished by harnessing the power for the Pareto principle.

The Pareto principle states that roughly 80 percent of effects come from 20 percent of the causes.[3] This principle highlights the observation, that a majority of results actually come from a minority of inputs. Management consultant guru Joseph Juran popularized the principle as the "80/20 rule" among Silicon Valley startups.

Throughout the last several decades, this 80/20 rule has been applied to a variety of business sectors, such as manufacturing, real estate, and venture-backed startups. The core thesis is that by only concentrating on "what matters" and ignoring everything else, businesses can produce more, increase their bottom lines, and make their customers happier.

Anyone who craves producing more with less has flocked to this idea.

The principle is also applicable to our daily lives and routines. The theory can be used in unexpected places, from your closet, to time spent with clients, to output at work, or even your finances.

By learning how to concentrate only on the essential tasks, you can free up space to do more of the things you love. From a financial perspective, you make hundreds of transitions every month. When you pause to analyze them through the lens of the Pareto principle, you start to see that not all expenses are created equal.

There are categories in which you spend a disproportionate amount of money and may not align with your passions. By honing in on these areas and eliminating them, you can stop spending on things that don't maximize your happiness. By aligning your monthly spending with your passions you capture the full power of the Pareto principle.

Passion Budgeting

If you enjoy things that bring you pleasure, then this section is for you.

This is probably the most pleasurable budgeting process on the planet. It begins with examining things in your life that bring you joy and ends with removing everything else. The passion budget focuses on optimizing your financial decisions so that you can pay off debt faster, save more, and get to the rich life. The passion budget helps you clean out the clutter in your financial life and frees up your decision-making to accelerate your path to budgeting bliss.

> "Americans spend $1.2 trillion annually on non-essential goods—in other words, items they do not need."
> —Joshua Becker[4]

Bestselling author and tidiness guru Marie Kondo has become an international sensation after building a massive movement centered around removing "clutter" from people's lives. In *The Life-Changing Magic of Tidying,* Kondo urges clients and readers who live clutter-filled lives to adopt a new outlook on the *things* that they own. She advocates that the items you possess should be judged through the lens of *passion.* The quantity of material possessions is not Kondo's focus, only the quality of passion the items elicit. In her philosophy, the test for passion is binary: Either the object sparks passion, or it does not. Kondo argues, "If the object sparks joy in your life, then keep it."[5]

Build a budget that sparks passion in your heart.

Passion budgeting uses the Pareto principle in a new way, because passion budgeting advocates that you should spend your money in areas that make you happy. Why hassle over pennies on purchases when you could strike directly at the core of your spending problems and absolve yourself of guilt when you do spend? However, in the areas that don't spark passion, you should cut your expenses ruthlessly. This is vital to long-term success.

This passion-centric approach to budgeting yields lasting results by examining the things that bring joy into your life. Follow these four steps to decipher what you need to focus on in your budget.

1. Investigate Your Expenses

The first step to passion budgeting is to assume that you are eliminating all of your expenses. Start with a clean slate. Then gradually add items back into your budget, but only those that spark joy or passion.

Don't get me wrong, everyone needs the essential elements of their budget (housing, food, transportation, and so on). The difference is that passion budgeting urges you to spend your money in proportion to your wants. In other words, focus your spending on the categories that matter the most to you. By assigning a weight and importance to each type of expense, you will be able to focus on what drives meaning in your life.

So, where do you begin?

The best predictor of future behavior is past behavior. Take a look at your bank and credit card statements from the last three months. With all of these statements in hand, grab a highlighter and mark the best purchases that you made throughout the last three months. This time frame gives you a clear view of your purchasing behaviors. The criterion for highlighting these purchases is simply whether those purchases sparked joy in your life. If so, then the purchase gets highlighted.

For example, if you love going out to eat, highlight all of the times you went out to dinner. Or if you enjoy working out, highlight your gym membership and any purchase associated with health. Once you are done highlighting, grab a black marker and circle every purchase that was not highlighted.

The chances are that you have a much larger part of your bank statement or credit card statement circled in black rather than highlighted items that spark joy. This is typical. People usually spend the most money on things that do not even matter to them.

2. Analyze Your Passion Categories

Now that you have a starting point for your new budget, it is time to take it one step further. Look at all of the items that you highlighted in Step 1 and group them into categories. Then assign a weight to each category (1 being the best and 6 being your least favorite). In the following chart there are six major expense categories for you to tally up all of your highlighted purchases. Additionally, it is important to summarize all of the expenses that you circled in black too. Go to MillennialMoneyMakeover.com to download your own passion categories spreadsheet.

Passion Categories	Total Count Highlighted	Passion Weight (1-6)
Housing	$3,000	5
Food	$2,700	1
Transportation	$600	4
Going out/fun	$900	3
Clothing	$400	2
Other	$700	6
Total Circled in Black	$900	Eliminate

After you have analyzed your expenses and summarized them by passion category, the next step is to select the top three areas in which you want to *continue* spending. These are most likely the top three weighted areas in your passion categories (in the example above—Food, Clothing, and Going out/fun). You should keep spending in these areas (although you might need to regulate total dollars spent) and reduce your spending in the bottom three weighted categories.

Next, take a look at the total amount that you circled in black. This is probably your most significant area for improvement. Investigating the consistency of these expenses will help you determine what to focus on. Sit down and analyze your spending behavior. It is essential to determine how much spending to eliminate in the areas that do not spark passion.

Once you choose an amount to cut, say $200, eliminate that sum from your monthly spending. Instead of spending that money on things that you don't care about, you can now put that $2,400 in annualized savings toward paying off a credit card, eliminating a student loan, building up your retirement nest egg, or investing.

3. Prioritize for Budgeting

You can't manage what you don't measure. Now that you have a clear view of your spending behavior, you need to incorporate this knowledge into building a budget and track your progress.

Don't make the same mistakes twice; when you start to create your budget, prioritize what makes you happy. If you are in debt and need to eliminate expenses in your life to allocate toward debt elimination, then cut the areas that you don't care about. If your goal is to save for a wedding or start a retirement account, the same strategy applies.

For now, take some time to prioritize what matters to you. The entire point of creating a budget is to give you an unobstructed view of the future. It is entirely up to you to take advantage of this opportunity.

4. Build a Passionate Income

Now that you have examined your expenses, it is critical to turn your attention to your income. Generating passion in *how* you make money is just as important as *spending* on things that make you happy.

Do you love your job? Does it spark passion into your life?

Be honest with yourself here. There should be joy in your work. The daily commute should not be dreaded. Instead, it should be something that cultivates purpose and joy. These are vital elements to a successful and long career. If your job sparks passion and happiness in your daily life, then you are one of the lucky few.

As Millennials, we are the most educated generation in history and we suffer from severe expectation dissonance. For many of us, when we finally made our way into the real world and began adulting, we realized the chasm between what was advertised for our profession and the reality of the daily grind. *This* is what a lawyer does? *This* is what an accountant does? *This* is how you sell insurance? *This* is how politics work?

We yearn for more. And if you can't find immediate passion in your current job, then focus on building up your resume in something that does spark joy, such as freelancing, a side hustle, or new business. By combining joy, interest, and purpose into your career, you will set yourself up to make more money in the long run.

Now that you understand the importance of incorporating passion into both your income and expenses, it is paramount that you maximize this theory. In the next section, you will work on actually creating your budget.

How to Budget Passionately

As of 2016, Millennials represent the largest generation in the United States workforce.[6] This means that the majority of people in their twenties and thirties are employees experiencing the art of business for the first time.

Managing your finances is much like running a business. For the vast majority of people, this means hardwiring a different type of approach to how you handle your money. As a participant in the real world, the time has come to control your life. And that begins with budgeting.

The act of creating a budget has an illuminating effect on your finances. The process can magnify areas for improvement and emphasize areas you are already dominating. As you will see, the basics of budgeting are quite simple, but the remainder is nuanced.

The first step is to list out all of your sources of income. Next, you will list out all of your expenses. You can use your passion expense categories as a reference point. Lastly, you will subtract your total expenses from your total income. You will either be left with a positive number (yes!) or a negative number (no!). Look at the example chart below to get an idea, then download a blank spreadsheet from MillennialMoneyMakeover.com and take a crack at it.

	Annual Budget	Monthly Budget
Income		
Salary (post tax)	$37,500	$3,125
Bonus (post tax)	$3,750	$313
Other incomes	$3,750	$313
Total income	$45,000*	$ 3,750
Expenses		
Rent	$12,000	$1,000
Food	$10,800	$900
Insurance	$1,800	$150
Utilities	$1,200	$100
Clothing	$1,800	$150

	Annual Budget	**Monthly Budget**
Cell phone	$1,200	$100
Credit card payments	$1,800	$150
Student loan payments	$5,400	$450
Transportation	$2,400	$200
Going out/fun	$3,600	$300
Miscellaneous	$2,100	$175
Total expenses	$44,100	$3,675
Net income	**$900**	**$75**

Assumes $50,000 salary, $5,000 bonus, $5,000 other income, and 25 percent tax rate

How did you do? If you got a positive number, then you are on the right path. But you will learn how to make this higher. If you had a negative mumber, don't panic—yet. This is an iterative process, and you will learn what areas to tweak to get to your goal.

Now that you have a holistic view of where you stand, it is time to dive into each component of your budget. Most financial coaches start by focusing on your income. But as you know, most people are pretty much locked into their current earnings, which makes it harder to adjust this number quickly. Although we will cover ways to increase your income, the fastest area of improvement lies in your expenses.

By focusing on restrictive behaviors, like reducing consumption, you can start seeing the results you want immediately. Not all expenses are the same, and it is incredibly important to know which ones to concentrate on.

In the next several sections, we are going to analyze expenses as a whole because focusing on this area of your budget can produce serious benefits, freeing up money to use in other areas. By applying a restrictive strategy to your expenses and maximizing your spend, you will be able to amplify your results.

Variable Vanities and Fixed Costs

There are two main types of costs in life: fixed costs and variable costs. Learning about each type will increase your financial acumen and give you a better understanding of which purchases to control. By learning which types of expenses cause a disproportionate amount of problems in your budget, you ignite the catalyst to your money makeover.

> "An important distinction is that rich people buy luxuries last, while the poor and middle class tend to buy luxuries first."
> —Robert Kiyosaki

Variable Vanities—Get a Grip

The beautiful thing about variable costs is that they are completely controllable. Variable costs are costs that rise and fall in proportion to the goods or services you consume. They vary from month to month and can include food, entertainment, utilities, clothing, and transportation.

For example, if you examine how much money you spent on clothing throughout the last six months, chances are you did not pay the exact same amount per month. Instead, you may have purchased new shoes one month, a bathing suit the next, and four shirts the following month.

Here is where dealing with variable costs gets fun. The costs that rise and fall the quickest are often the most *unnecessary*. Sure, you may *want* new shoes, but do you really *need* them?

Overall, cutting variable costs is a crucial element to success when you are trying to improve other areas of your financial life, such as making higher debt payments, building a savings fund, or purchasing investments.

Eliminating life down to the studs is not a successful approach to create sound financial habits. Small pleasures make up our day. For example, I love coffee. There is no way I would ever eliminate my morning espresso consumption. Although my monthly Nespresso bill is directly correlated with my espresso consumption, it is a cost I will never remove because I would not be happy in my money makeover. Marrying the things you enjoy in life with your budget is critical for long-term success. That is where passion budgeting comes in; cut the costs that you don't care about.

Fixed Costs—Keep Them Low

Fixed costs are the exact opposite of variable costs. By definition, fixed costs are expenses that are not dependent on the consumption level of a certain set of goods or services. They tend to be longer-term and have a set contracted amount. They can include your rent or mortgage, a monthly gym membership, student loans, or car notes.

Although variable costs offer the opportunity to pick the low-hanging fruit from your budget, fixed costs are where the high expenses reside. If you can adjust these to acceptable levels, you will disproportionately affect your budget.

Let me give you a real-world example. When I moved from New York City to Austin, I was able to cut my rent by more than 45 percent, while at the same time keeping everything else in my finances constant—income and variable costs. This simple adjustment alone freed up more than $500 per month in my budget. Imagine what you could do with $500 extra dollars a month for one year: save six times as much as the average American, pay off 20 percent of the average student loan, or eliminate the average Millennial credit card debt.

If you aim to accrue financial intelligence and change the behaviors that genuinely matter, then you need to focus your efforts. Hone in on the major players in your life: fixed costs. Worrying about eliminating small expenses, which erode your happiness, is not an effective strategy. This may not be the traditional approach, but it is essential to determine what truly impacts your money.

Happy Spending

Now that you have learned how to build a budget and determine the types of costs to keep, it is essential to examine how to maximize your spending. In this section, we will examine *how* to best spend money. It turns out what we spend our money on can make us feel richer and more fulfilled. This is the fun part.

In their groundbreaking book *Happy Money—The Science of Happier Spending*, psychologist Elizabeth Dunn and Harvard Business School professor Michael Norton examined a curious question: Does the way in which we spend our money affect our happiness? The answer is: absolutely.

Dunn and Norton found that spending your money in the five following ways can increase your financial outlook.[7]

1. *Buying experiences:* This principle is driven by the premise that buying experiences over material purchases is better in the long run. The novelty of new purchases tends to wear off over time, while experiences such as a vacation with family or a concert with friends can be mentally revisited over and over, thus allowing the consumer to extract more pleasure from the purchase.

2. *Making it a treat:* Do you love dining out and trying new restaurants? Instead of eating out every week, make it a treat and reward yourself only after a major accomplishment. Once you receive that promotion, hit that goal, or earn that annual bonus, then and only then, splurge on going to that swanky new restaurant. This strategy will make the happiness of the purchase last longer and ties a positive memory to the reward.

3. *Buying time:* Let's face it. We are all a little selfish. Buying time allows us to do what we want when we want. If you love reading but your house is a complete disaster, then hiring a maid to clean while you enjoy your book is a fantastic use of capital. This decision creates the needed time for you to read and simultaneously completes a household chore. This concept is life-changing.

4. *Paying first and consuming later:* Credit cards have turned the traditional payment sequence upside down. Today, the mantra is to consume first and pay later. But prepaying draws on the idea that paying early, and with cash, increases the pain of the transaction and places the pain *before* consumption. By prepaying, we bask in anticipation of the purchase

longer, thereby drawing a longer mental value from the purchase.

5. *Investing in others:* Helping those in need is a core value of the American way of life. We are taught at an early age that sharing, giving gifts, and making charitable contributions is the responsible thing to do. It turns out following this advice can make our wallets feel heavier. The act of giving makes us feel more affluent and increases our overall well-being.

We all have to spend money. So, we might as well do it intelligently. By focusing on the five ways to increase our happiness through spending, you can leverage your budget to your advantage. Remember these principles as you progress throughout the budgeting process and the rewards will be twofold: financial health and increased happiness.

Financial Rules of Thumb: Myth vs. Reality

To determine whether you are in line with good financial practices or incredibly off base, the finance industry has provided rules of thumb. These rules are distributed in an attempt to give you a baseline of comparison and keep your costs under control. The problem is that these rules are wildly generic and offer terrible advice. There are three of them that I'd like to tackle head-on.

Debt Myth: Your debt payments should not exceed 20 percent of your take-home pay. The implicit assumption in this rule is that it is acceptable to finance your lifestyle. That drives me crazy. This rule allows you to allocate a substantial portion of your take-home pay to finance credit card debt, student loans, or consumer debt. The issue is that the average college graduate will have $37,172 in student loans and some credit card debt sprinkled on top of this as well.[8] Based on the average graduating salary, the average debt payments are already approaching, if not exceeding, 20 percent of take-home pay, which is a financial disaster.

Debt Reality: Once you become debt free, you should remain debt free. After paying off all of your debt you should stay in the black, plain and simple. The *controllable* debt in your life should be eliminated. The only true exception here is a mortgage, which we will discuss in Chapter 4. Because your primary goal should be to alleviate yourself from debt completely, there is no turning back to debt after you have completed your money makeover.

....

Housing Myth: Your housing payments should not exceed 30 percent of your take-home pay. The problem with any standard is that human behavior migrates to the mean. People will get too close to this standard, if not exceed it. Setting the standard housing payment—rent or mortgage—at 30 percent of your take-home pay is ludicrous. The problem is that housing will be your highest fixed cost *and* it is a long-term commitment. Your goal should be to keep this as low as comfortably possible.

Housing Reality: Your housing payments should not exceed 20 percent of your take-home pay. Keeping your housing cost at or below 20 percent will free up the necessary cash in your budget to construct a healthy ecosystem—paying off debt, building up a savings cushion, investing to grow your wealth, and stashing away cash for retirement. You cannot complete all of these necessary things at the appropriate rate by spending more than 20 percent of your take-home pay on rent.

Now, before we move on, I want to address everyone in the peanut gallery: *What about New York, Los Angeles, Chicago, and Boston? It is impossible to spend just 20 percent of your take-home income on rent!*

This is a makeover, and if you want to expedite your path to financial freedom, then you need to consider moving to a city where you can afford to live. If you live in a city that eats up more than 20 percent of your discretionary income solely on rent, it is time to make some hard choices. This is not a book on how to stay in the rat race. This is a book about jumping off the wheel and finding the richness of life.

There is good news though. Once you have built up enough savings, you can move back to these cities. Geographic arbitrage is very real and tangible. Take advantage of this.

....

Savings Myth: Your savings should be at least 15 percent of your take-home pay. This rule is not as bad as the rest because at least it advocates saving. But 15 percent will not get you where you want to go. If you have read this far, I know that you are "all in" on the money makeover. Although 15 percent will get your savings headed in the right direction, you will need to crank this up as soon as possible.

Savings Reality: Your savings should be at least 30 percent of your take-home pay. The fact that you are saving means that you are ahead of your peers. By saving at least 30 percent of your take-home pay (once you are done paying off your debt), you will be speeding down the highway to riches. As that 30 percent begins to accumulate you will find that the worries you had before suddenly begin to disappear.

Saving, and then investing, is the quickest way to cross the money makeover finish line. Ratchet this number up as high as you can and automate this decision (more on this in Chapter 6).

When you are setting up your passion budget, it will be important to allocate where you are spending your money correctly. If you are leveraging the *Happy Money* principles and looking for places to optimize your spending, this can be a painless and fun process. There will be areas where you can cut and others where you can splurge. The important point is to focus on getting the biggest bang for your buck.

....

The rules of thumb are exactly that—standard. Your money makeover is anything but standard. The process of financially redefining yourself requires a change in perspective. Adopt the money makeover rules of thumb, and they will serve you well.

Socioeconomic Downsizing

Financial success can be engineered. The problem is that the equation runs dangerously juxtaposed to our ingrained social values of consumption and hyper spending. In a world run by Facebook, Instagram, and Snapchat, it is far too easy to be lured into the false assumption that everyone is in the one percent. Social media exacerbates this notion, and as a result, we are always worried about the fear of missing out.

Raised in a world where having the latest phone, car, or clothes is the proverbial choice, it comes as no surprise that savings and delayed gratification are becoming extinct concepts. However, the key to getting ahead financially is to embrace these generationally archaic concepts by *socioeconomic downsizing*.

"Live like no one else today so you can live like no one else tomorrow."
—Dave Ramsey

By definition, socioeconomic downsizing is the active choice to live one or two rungs lower on the economic ladder than your current income allows. Let's look at an example.

Jane and Bob, a happily married couple from Dallas, each earn $50,000. With a combined total household income of $100,000, they are in the top 28 percent of household incomes. They have two choices: to live high on the hog or to socioeconomically downsize. They choose the latter. With this choice comes a significant adjustment in lifestyle. Their discretionary spending on rent, food, and fun changes drastically. This choice to downsize completely alters their day-to-day life.

Instead of living in the nicest part of town, paying a monthly rent of $1,100 (or roughly 20 percent of their monthly take-home pay) the couple will pay $550 if they choose to downsize. Instead of spending $600 per month on financing new cars, Jane and Bob will drive cars they own if they choose to downsize. Instead of taking two ski vacations this year, they will embrace a staycation if they choose to downsize.

So, why would anyone choose this masochistic path?

The answer is: This choice allows Bob to save his yearly salary of $50,000. After three short years the couple will accumulate $150,000 in savings, or 1.5 times their household income. As the emergency fund, slush fund, and retirement savings begin to build, Jane and Bob can start the process of shopping for their dream house, purchase new cars, or start saving for their children's college tuition. They have already put in the sacrifice *early* to accumulate their *base* savings. The couple can now take enjoyment in watching their investments grow for the rest of their lives. For them, the hard part will already be over.

Now that we have sufficiently covered how to stretch your spending and analyzed strategies for boosting your happiness along the way, it is time to turn your attention to the top line of your budget: income. Increasing your income can alleviate the stress of managing an anemic monthly cash flow. The first step is to determine how you measure against your peers, and then contemplate how to leverage your existing skills and assets to garner more income.

Where Do You Stand?

Comparison offers a proxy for reality. Knowing where your salary stands among your peers gives you the ability to see how on or off track you are trending. In their groundbreaking book *The Millionaire Next Door,* professors Thomas Stanley and William Danko establish the positive correlation between high incomes and the ability to generate wealth. Intuitively, this makes perfect sense—the higher your income, the more money you can put toward saving and investing. Of course, this only happens if you can avoid the pitfall of amassing high levels of debt because you think your high salary will fuel your spending machine.

"I don't care what anyone says. Being rich is a good thing."
—Marc Cuban

In the long run, your ability to increase your income can have a significant impact on your ability to pay off debt, generate needed savings, and fuel your desired lifestyle. Knowing where you stand among your peers can give you the relative insight into how well you are performing.

Luckily, with data collected from a 2015 survey, *Business Insider* can give you that needed glimpse. From the survey data, *Business Insider* calculated the income levels necessary to be in the top 50 percent and the top 1 percent of Millennial earners. The results might make you seriously reexamine your earnings.

At the young end of the spectrum, the data found that a twenty-five-year-old worker needed an income of $31,000 to be in the top 50 percent of earners, while an income of $116,000 was necessary to reach the top 1 percent.

As you might expect, the income numbers continued to climb in direct correlation with the age of the Millennial worker. In the middle of the data, a thirty-year-old worker needed to generate $40,000 to be in the top 50 percent, while a whopping $173,000 of income was required to reach the top 1 percent. This trend continued with their older counterparts, who at thirty-five-years-old needed an income of $45,000 to remain in the top 50 percent but a staggering income of $291,000 was necessary to earn a spot in the top 1 percent.[9]

So, where do you stand?

If you feel behind, don't freak out. There are plenty of ways to increase your income, all of which you can start working toward today. This might mean gunning for that promotion at work, starting your own business, or freelancing.

Readers might find themselves in the top income brackets but don't feel rich at all. This is because they are not *living* the rich life. Proper money management does not increase with financial position. The "just in time" lifestyle is just as dangerous for the janitor as for the judge. If your salary increases and financial literacy remains constant, then your problems will only grow in size.

Wherever you fall on the income chart, it is important to keep in mind that although increasing your income is highly correlated with long-term wealth, it does not guarantee financial success. How you handle your money is just as important as how much you earn.

Increasing your income has tremendous benefits on your ability to pay off debt, accumulate savings, and start investing. Let's examine a few ways to upgrade your lifestyle.

From Side Hustlers to Entrepreneurs

Philip Taylor is a successful entrepreneur, writer, and businessman. Nick Loper is a podcast extraordinaire, TEDx alumni, and Chief Side Hustler at Side Hustle Nation. Nicole Lapin is a television host and bestselling author. They didn't all start this way.

This section is dedicated to showing you real-world success stories of people who have turned their quest for more money in their budget into full-time, and highly profitable, careers.

PT Money

In April 2007, Philip Taylor made a purchase that would alter the course of his life: his blog domain name. Since that day, Taylor—or PT Money, as most of his readership knows him—has become a sensation in the personal finance community.

A certified public accountant by trade, Taylor was working as an internal auditor in a corporate environment and making six figures. But something wasn't quite right.

Like most young professionals, Taylor was working to get his finances in order and was reading vigorously on the topic of money. But at that moment, in the calm of corporate life, Taylor decided to "quit consuming and start creating."[10] He wanted to become part of the financial conversation.

After starting his personal finance blog, PTmoney.com, Taylor's efforts started paying off. Within a couple years, Taylor was making $40,000 from blogging (in addition to his corporate salary), and he was beginning to put his newfound cash to good use.

"I was using that extra money to get my finances in order. I was paying off consumer debt with the extra cash and starting to get operationally lean in my daily expenses,"[11] said Taylor. Taylor's success came in the form of a two-pronged approach. Step one was to generate extra cash from his new side business, and step two was to cut expenses simultaneously. The formula worked.

Two years after launching PTmoney.com, Taylor made the leap from corporate life to full-time entrepreneur. Since then, Taylor has developed a strong following among his readers and his website has millions of page views a year.

I asked Taylor what advice he would give to readers who want to turn a side business into a full-time opportunity. "Get your finances in the best shape possible. Be as lean and mobile as you can," says Taylor. "Business is not about the 'me versus them' attitude. Instead, work with your competition as collaborators. Go find the people who have done what you want to do—set goals, set expectations, and move forward."[12]

Although Taylor has already found his success, he still thinks the Internet is wide open with opportunity. The only question is: Who will seize the moment?

Nick Loper

In his 2014 TEDx talk, Nick Loper delivered an unorthodox message. Playing to an older crowd, Loper gave the audience a sound bite they wanted to hear: Millennials are entitled. What the crowd didn't expect was Loper's new twist on the subject.

His message was: Yes, Millennials are entitled. They are entitled to the pursuit of their dreams, and our future economy fundamentally depends on Millennials' unprecedented pursuit of entrepreneurship. Loper is speaking from first hand experience.

In 2005, Loper was stuck in a sales job with Ford Motor Company that wasn't sparking passion. Assigned to meeting monthly sales quotas, Loper yearned for a creative outlet. After some experimentation, Loper created his first successful online business, and from that point, his days at Ford were numbered. He has since gone on to develop several successful online companies, his most noteworthy being Side Hustle Nation. As "Chief Side Hustler" at Side Hustle Nation, Loper has dedicated himself to helping others turn their part-time passion projects into full-time employment.

His *Side Hustle Show* podcast, which has been running weekly since 2013, boasts a burgeoning collection of notable guests. A typical show might include a quest to find out how other people bring their business from $0 to $50,000 a month, like Michelle Schroeder-Gardner of Making Sense of Cents, or how successful founders of multi-million-dollar businesses get their start, like Noah Kagan, the founder of Sumo. Loper's audience loves hearing about real-world people creating, growth hacking, and building their way to profitable businesses. The numbers speak for themselves.

The *Side Hustle Show* has more than five million downloads. What started as a passion project for Loper has morphed into a successful business. In an interview with Loper, I asked what advice he would give to those trying to make more money with their side project. Loper reminded me that everyone starts at the same point: zero. Loper emphasized, "The best opportunities aren't visible until you are in motion. The practice of getting started leads to new opportunities."[13]

The only direction, it seems, is up.

Nicole Lapin

Among the offices of CNN and CNBC, Nicole Lapin is the youngest anchor ever at both networks.[14] Lapin cut her teeth early, and that experience has paid dividends for her career.

Lapin leveraged her early start covering business news and is already starring as the host of the business show *Hatched* on the CW, a show dedicated to connecting emerging brands with successful mentors.

When Lapin isn't helping entrepreneurs turn their businesses into success stories, she is working on her other side projects. And those projects have been tremendously successful.

Lapin is the author of two bestselling books, *Rich Bitch* and *Boss Bitch*. Her breakout book *Rich Bitch,* a personal finance guide for women, made the *New York Times* Best Sellers list.[15] So, she doubled down on the momentum and started writing a syndicated personal finance column for *Redbook Magazine*.

After the initial success of her debut book, Lapin did the unexpected and churned out another bestseller, *Boss Bitch.* This book focuses on taking charge of your life and offers advice for women in their careers and personal lives.[16]

....

All three of these entrepreneurs embody the rewarding principles of the money makeover on their journey toward financial and career success. The workman-like approach to chasing their dreams, while simultaneously increasing their income, should serve as inspiration. You can always find ways to push the boundaries of your career, life, and budget.

If you need extra cash to help expedite paying off your credit cards, student loans, or building up your savings accounts, then I have good news. We live in an age of online businesses, the sharing economy, and many other accessible opportunities. The process of making more money has never been easier.

....

Money Makeover Pro Tip:
How to Make More Money Quickly

When trying to make more money, look at extracting value from assets you already own:

- Housing: Airbnb or VRBO

- Transportation: Uber or Lyft

- Appliances: eBay or Craigslist

- Intellectual capital: Flexjobs or Skooli

....

How to Ask for a Raise

If you feel like you aren't making enough money, you are in good company. According to a 2016 analysis of Federal Reserve data, Millennials are earning a whopping 20 percent less than their parents at the same stage in life.[17] With systemic economic problems diffusing into the daily lives of millions of Millennials, young professionals feel behind.

If you feel overworked and undercompensated, there might be more money lurking right under your nose. Asking for a raise might be a great way for you to earn more money and simultaneously establish career momentum. But just asking for a raise could be damaging to your relationships in the workplace. Instead, you need to develop a winning strategy. Asking for a raise can feel intimidating, so build up your confidence by taking four concrete steps to solidify your raise.

1. Determine Exactly What You Want

The art of negotiating a raise begins with some self-reflection. If you are building up your confidence to ask for a raise, then you must have a reason. Are you feeling overworked? Do you think you deserve a promotion? Are you getting equal pay for equal work?

At the core of your desire to ask for a raise, something is troubling you. You need to use this opportunity to identify the issue. If you think you deserve a promotion, then you need to demonstrate your case in a clear and concise manner. If you want a 10 percent increase in salary, then you need to articulate how you go above and beyond your current job description.

It is critical to be as specific as you can when developing your goal. Pinpointing your "ask" will allow you to construct a roadmap to achieving your goal.

2. Develop Your Plan

With your goal now formalized you have something to aim toward. The problem is always "How do I get from A to B?" First, you should take a deep breath and realize that whatever you are trying to accomplish has already been done before.

If you are gunning for a promotion, then examine the job description of the position you are pursuing. What are the baseline criteria? Have you achieved them all already? If you have, then you need to do it again, but this time with your boss noticing. If you have not met this baseline, then you need to figure out how to incorporate those new skills into your daily work. Give yourself time to strive toward your goal. Write down three things that you can improve upon over the next three months.

Let's say you are an account manager. Your first month's goal could be to get a handle on all of your existing accounts. The second month could be replicating the first month's efficiencies plus landing a new client. The third month may be doing everything in the first and second months and additionally mentoring junior account associates. In three short months, you will have developed great rapport with your accounts, gained new business, and demonstrated your management ability.

3. Set an Ask Date

Asking for a raise without coming to the table with tangible results is a terrible idea. So if you need more than three months, then you should take the time to meet your objectives. However, once you are ready, showing up to a meeting with a list of accomplishments will speak volumes about your skill set and what you have to offer.

While working on establishing your list of accomplishments, map out a timeline of when you want to ask for your raise or promotion. I suggest doing this well before your company's typical mid-year and year-end review periods.

The reason you don't want to have this critical conversation during your regular compensation meeting is that the decision about your future has already been made. The executive suite has already determined who will get raises and promotions. Showing enthusiasm and drive *before* these meetings will allow your superiors to advocate on your behalf *during* performance evaluation meetings.

Understanding the timing of when to present your reasons for advancement is almost as important as the reasons themselves. As they say, timing is everything.

4. Deliver and Get Feedback

Once you have set your ask date, the last thing to do before your meeting is to write down your expected outcome. This will give you a clear means to decide if you received the answer you wanted, especially after the fog of the conversation evaporates. Otherwise, there is no way to determine whether you were successful or not.

After you have your meeting, it will be important to examine the result. Did you get what you asked for? Was it better or worse than you expected? Did your receive a contingent answer?

Whatever the result, write down exactly what happened. This will serve as an excellent reference for future negotiations. If something did not work, then maybe you need to adjust a variable to make the conversation more successful.

Asking for a raise can be a crucial part of career development. Your bosses may not realize how hard you are working. They might take you for granted. They might happily give you a raise. Either way, the important thing is that you asked. That is a win.

By bolstering your income, you will be well on the way to developing a more sophisticated budget. The next step to building a passion budget is to make sure you are adopting the right processes to win over the long term. These processes and maxims will serve as guiding forces as you scale your success.

Adopting a Savings Process

After optimizing your budget to increase your income and leverage your spending, it will also be crucial to build savings into your routine. Defining how much you want to save ties back into your goal-setting from Chapter 1.

"Don't save what is left after spending; spend what is left after saving."
—Warren Buffet

For example, if your goal is to buy your first car, then you need to calculate a total savings goal. Knowing this total goal allows you to deconstruct your overall savings goal into yearly, monthly, or weekly components. Meeting these intermittent goals dramatically increases your chances of overall goal achievement.

The following tips can help you improve your odds at accumulating those small wins.

1. Pay Yourself First

If you are like most people, the end of the month leaves you scratching your head, wondering where all of your money went. The typical process goes something like this: Your paycheck comes in, the monthly bills are paid, and you save (if you are lucky) what is left over. This is a poor way to accumulate savings.

The cable bill, rent, utilities, and car payment all come before your savings goals. This haphazard way of managing your finances prioritizes paying expenses above savings and yields low results. My guess is that this method has not worked for you either.

To meet your savings goals, you need to readjust the order of operations and start paying yourself *first*. When your paycheck comes in, your savings goal should be deducted first. Everyone else who has a claim on your money can wait.

Without the critical decision to prioritize your savings, you will always feel like you are underachieving. Stop the cycle of under accumulating by paying yourself first.

2. Automate Your Savings

Once you start paying yourself first, the next step is to automate the process. By automating how much to save, you increase the probability of meeting your savings goals and simultaneously remove the temptation to spend your savings.

The best way to automate your savings decision is to make the decision once and apply the "set it and forget it" method. Most payroll providers have the ability to directly deposit funds into a separate account *before* your paycheck hits your primary bank account. If you are not sure if your payroll provider has this function, then consult with your human resources department. The alternative is to set up automatic deductions from your bank account to your savings account. Both methods are highly effective.

Ultimately, the trick is never to see your *savings* enter your *spending* account or, at the very least, have it stay there for as little time as possible. By not ever seeing the money in your spending account, you feel no attachment toward the money. As a result, your savings are left alone to accumulate.

3. Save Extra Pay

As you read earlier, our economy has endless ways to make more money. Whether you increase your pay through the traditional path of career progression or find successful side hustles, putting your newfound wealth into savings will expedite your ride to the rich life.

By making the decision to put all extra money into your savings, you alleviate the income trap. The income trap theory is: When you earn more money, you tend to spend more money. This is a philosophy of the financially unhealthy. The issue with the income trap is that as incomes rise, so too do the size of financial mistakes.

The best way to protect yourself from these mistakes is to preemptively allocate your savings by automating the decision. By doing this, you will not feel the temptation to start spending your extra income. Of course, all work and no play is an unhealthy recipe. You should treat yourself occasionally while still keeping your savings momentum going.

4. Track Your Progress

Metrics matter, so it is important to monitor your performance. While you don't need to track your progress daily, it is essential to keep a regular pulse. After all, there is a reason that you are working hard to save your money. A fun and effective way to track your goals is to name your savings accounts. For example:

- Down payment on our first house
- Honeymoon fund to Thailand
- Wedding and bachelorette parties
- Annual ski trip to Vail

Research conducted by Dr. Brad Klontz of Creighton University found that naming your savings accounts could dramatically increase the odds of meeting your savings goals.[18] Have some fun during the naming process and make the names memorable. By tracking your progress and assigning purposeful names, your intentions will eventually turn into reality.

Everyone wants more savings. Even affluent people worry about not saving enough. You can mitigate this worry by identifying your savings goals, remembering to pay yourself first, and automating that decision. This series of decisions will catapult you toward success. Finally, don't forget to track your progress and have some fun along the way.

In the following table, find your savings goal amount in the left column and the corresonding savings needed to reach your goal based on the time frame you select in the top row.

Monthly Savings Goals			
	Savings Time Frame		
Annualized Goal	1 Year	5 Years	10 Years
$1,000	$83	$17	$8
$5,000	$417	$83	$42
$15,000	$1,250	$250	$125
$20,000	$1,668	$333	$167
$25,000	$2,083	$417	$208
$50,000	$4,167	$833	$417
$100,000	$8,333	$1,678	$833
*Savings goals are calculated on a per month basis, ignoring the time value of money.			

Action Items

An entire chapter on budgeting is a necessary stop on your money makeover. Your financial transformation begins with gaining a holistic view of your financial life. This is often the most resisted, but eye-opening, part of any money makeover. The truth can be an unforgiving teacher.

When creating your budget, remember the following lessons and harness the power of passion budgeting.

1. Build a passion budget that works.

2. Focus on keeping things in your life that spark passion.

3. Understand the expenses that control your budget.

4. Make more money; it helps everything.

5. Understand that your budget is a living document.

The entire point of creating a budget is to give you insight. The money makeover is about taking that knowledge and applying it *purposefully*. The information gained from the exercises in this chapter will give you the knowledge, tools, and insights for continuous improvement.

In the next chapter, you will boost your financial mastery even further by learning how to best purchase large-ticket items and position yourself for decades of financial success. I encourage you to put yourself, and your budget, in your stretch zone. That is where the real growth begins.

4

THE MAGIC OF WINNING BIG: HOW TO OPTIMIZE LARGE-TICKET PURCHASES

Life is too short to be little.
—Disraeli

Richmond, Virginia, is a cozy city nestled along the I-95 corridor. Formerly one of the prizes of the South, the city has not hosted anything big these days. But at the University of Richmond, there is a group of professors who live for big things, especially large numbers.

Intrigued by recent public discourse happening in neighboring Washington, DC, professors David Landy, Noah Silber, and Aleah Goldin set out on a journey to understand the psychology of large numbers. They noticed that politicians and business leaders routinely discuss numbers such as millions, billions, and trillions in the public forum. But, the professors wondered, how well does the public synthesize these numbers? Do people treat these numbers equally? Do people have a healthy appreciation for numbers of this magnitude? Do people have the capacity to compare large numbers?

The researchers conducted a study entitled *Estimating Large Numbers*. The results of their study were enlightening.

An excerpt from the study discussed participants estimating numbers on a number line and revealed that "35% of participants in the study reported here . . . seem to evaluate large numbers on the assumption that the number labels pick out roughly equally spaced magnitudes as the numbers increased."[1]

This means that people had an extraordinarily difficult time estimating the right spacing between large numbers, say between one hundred million and four trillion. The size and scale of large numbers seemed lost on participants, especially as the numbers increased in size.

For life's large-ticket purchases, such as buying a car, purchasing an engagement ring, paying for a wedding, or acquiring your first house, people tend to get lost in the numbers. And it's not their fault. Large numbers have a very clever way of manipulating our brains. The abstract nature of their magnitude distorts their size.

If you are like most people, it is difficult to comprehend the value of $500,000 or $1,000,000. This is simply because you do not have very many immediate experiences with transactions of this scale, which leaves you with no point for relative comparison.

We continuously experience small numbers throughout the day. It is quite less frequent that we meet large numbers, and as a result they are harder for us to conceptualize. According to Daniel Ansari, a researcher at the Numerical Cognition Laboratory at Western University in Canada, "Our cognitive systems are very much tied to our perceptions."[2] And as we all know, our perceptions become our reality. The difficulty lies when we start thinking about numbers outside of our daily familiarity. "The main obstacle is that we're dealing with numbers that are too large for us to have experienced perceptually."[3] Large numbers are incredibly hard for our brains to grasp.

Our brains understand this deficiency and have adapted to deal with small numbers very well. For large numbers, we fall into the trap of rounding and estimating. The problem is that the scale of the rounding and estimating increases drastically as the numbers increase, furthering the distortion.

This is when most people make massive mistakes. In this chapter, you are going to learn how to avoid the costly mistakes of making purchases that are too large. You will learn to fight your brain's willingness to convert the non-linear to the linear.

To combat this problem, the professors at the University of Richmond suggest a strategy that translates the unfamiliar to the familiar: Convert large numbers into familiar units. For example, if you are used to dealing in hundred-dollar increments, then convert everything into the hundreds unit. That means $1,700 becomes 17 hundreds. Or $10,000 becomes 100 hundreds.

Use this technique when you are about to make a large purchase. And to make this even more powerful, set your baseline metric at your current savings or investments total. Therefore, if you have $5,000 in your savings account, purchasing a new car for $45,000 is nine times the value of your savings account. This allows for proportionate comparison.

Before you make your purchase, ask yourself: How long did it take to save $5,000? Is paying nine times your savings worth it for this car? These questions reset your mental frame of comparison and allow you to convert the abstract into the reality of known numbers.

This is a secret tool of the rich. And it is instrumental in leading the rich life.

This method is not taught in school nor does is come innately. Instead, it is acquired over time. Some people learn it from observing successful people, others through the drudgery of self-experience.

Learning how to optimize large-ticket purchases is a learned skill set, which will be the difference between long-term financial success and failure. The decisions you make about how much to spend on a new car, an engagement ring, your wedding, or your first house can drastically alter your financial health.

Hang on, because this might be the most crucial chapter yet.

Large-Ticket Purchase 1: Buying a Car

On a brisk September day in 2015, I rushed out of my apartment. The night before I had spent hours scouring the Internet for the best local car deals and had dialed in on my new ride. The new car smell was already in my mind.

As I headed to the dealership, the mounting intoxication of the purchase started to pulse through my body. As I sauntered into the showroom, a salesman (whom we will call "Jeff" for purposes of this book), instantly greeted me. Jeff was smiling wide, adopting the classic car salesman's tool of mimicry because, as we greeted, I caught myself grinning from ear to ear.

As we shook hands, my high started to fade. Reality seized me, and I understood that I was in enemy territory. Car salesmen, I reminded myself, are notoriously slick. They are to be watched with caution. I didn't want this schmoozer trying to sell me something I didn't need.

With my research complete, all I needed Jeff to do was facilitate the test drive. As Jeff and I were approaching the car, he threw me the keys. It was like a scene out of a movie, and I was playing the part.

Compared to my fourteen-year-old Suburban, the new car was like a spaceship, decked out with the platinum package: rearview cameras, GPS, automatic steering, heated seats, smooth leather, and gadgets galore. I was falling in love.

As we headed back to the dealership, I launched into a barrage of questions about the car's capabilities. Jeff answered each one in meticulous detail, furthering the appeal. But pulling back into the dealership, I noticed a curious sensation. A little voice was starting to chirp in my ear, "Ask him how much it is already!" I obliged. Jeff reported, "$40,000."

The last twelve months of dedicated savings started to flash before my eyes. Had all of that effort culminated into this one purchase? Did it make *sense* to buy a new car? Maybe I only needed a used one?

Suddenly, I didn't feel quite right. I got the immediate sensation that I needed to escape. I realized that every minute I spent in the car was a minute closer to purchasing the damn thing.

I told Jeff he would have my decision by the end of the week. To assuage the look he threw my way, I gave him my email address and told him to send me the specifics of the deal. I reassured him we would be in touch. (Yeah, right.)

Jeff had lost the deal. And he knew it. So, as punishment, he emailed me for months.

Luckily, I escaped the claws of a horrible financial mistake. All of my hard-earned savings would have been gone. And financial insecurity would have strolled right back into my life. Learning to delay immediate gratification is a learned behavior. I was starting to get my practice in that day. It was a small victory on a long journey.

Marshmallows, Pretzels, and Used Cars

In the fall of 1972, on the beautifully manicured campus of Stanford University, a curious thing was happening in a room with a double-sided mirror. A child was sitting at a table, glancing back and forth between a marshmallow and a pretzel. To the child's delight, he could have whichever one he wanted. It was approaching decision time: a marshmallow or a pretzel?

A couple of years earlier, on the same immaculate campus, social psychologists Walter Mischel and Ebbe Ebbesen were working on an experiment that tested the nature of delayed gratification. They were curious as to how people would react when rewards were placed directly in front of them. The researchers theorized that by placing a noticeable reward in front of someone (think Reese's, M&M's, or a Snickers), that person would be very good at waiting patiently to consume their reward. The researchers hypothesized that an increase in delayed gratification would occur because people would engage in "self-persuasion and anticipatory gratification."[4] At the time, that logic made perfect sense. As it turns out, the opposite was true.

In an experiment to test this hypothesis, children were either exposed to a reward or they weren't. The study revealed that the children who were given the option to consume their reward early did so, but the children not exposed to a reward ended up waiting longer to receive one.

This confirmed the "out of sight, out of mind" mentality.

Curiously though, researchers noticed that the children who were trying desperately not to consume their reward, when it was placed directly in front of them, engaged in "covert and overt distracting responses."[5] These kids were trying to distract themselves mentally or physically from consuming their reward, albeit with limited success.

Picking up on this observation, Mischel and Ebbesen conjured up a means to test a new hypothesis: "Overt activities and internal cognition and fantasy which would help the subject to distract himself from the reward would increase the length of time which he would delay gratification."[6]

Would they be wrong—again?

With a group of fifty children, the researchers tested their new hypothesis. In this experiment, children were given the choice of a delicious reward: a marshmallow or a pretzel. Then the children were told the researcher was going to leave the room. If the children waited until the researcher returned, the child would be able to eat their preferred reward. If they decided to bring the researchers back into the room, they would have to eat something else.

The children in this experiment were split into three groups. The first group, upon walking into a room and selecting which reward they wanted (marshmallow or pretzel) were cued to play with a slinky. The second group, after choosing their reward, was primed to think of something "fun" as a means of distraction. And finally, the third group was given no activity. They just had to wait.

The results were fascinating. For the group that was provided no means of distraction, the mean wait time was a mere 30 seconds before bringing the researcher back. By contrast, the group with the slinky reached a mean wait time of 8.59 minutes. What was even more surprising was the result of the third group. Those children who were told to think of something fun achieved a mean wait time of 12.12 minutes![7]

So what do the results tell us about human behavior? Well, for one, we are terrible at waiting for a prize when we have no means of distraction. However, if we can distract ourselves with activities like going on walks, runs, hiking, or reading, our resistance can be quite impressive. Additionally, if we can mentally distract ourselves from what we want, we can delay consumption even further. The temptation to eat our life's marshmallow ebbs away if we can adequately distract ourselves.

Six Things to Consider When Buying a Car

Adults are essentially large children. It stands to reason that if we want to consume, purchase, or acquire something beyond our financial means, the best way to combat our impulse is to use distraction techniques. But sometimes circumstance requires us to take the plunge.

Whether your current car broke down, an accident left you carless, or you are a first-time car buyer, you might just need to buy a car. The good news is car designers, manufactures, and salesmen don't quite know what to think of Millennials. They know that we value individualism, trust the experience of our peers, are optimistic, and are technology savvy. This puts us in the power seat.

Use this knowledge, as well as the following six rules, to get the best deal possible for your car.

1. Don't Buy New

Transportation is essential. Whether you are in a big city, suburb, or farm town, how you get around can change your financial outlook. For the money makeover expert, keeping transportation costs low is a key component of economic progress, especially for young professionals.

Before we get too far, I want to make one thing clear: A new car is not an investment. It is an expense. Resisting the temptation to purchase a new vehicle is difficult, especially after years of working hard. Naturally, you want something to show for it. Fight this impulse.

On average, a new car loses about 10 percent of its value the moment you leave the car dealership and another 10 percent by the end of the first year.[8] Let this simmer for a moment. If you were to fall to the siren song and purchase a $40,000 BMW, the *second* the tires leave the dealership, you have lost $4,000 in value.

A car is a depreciating asset, which means it declines in value over time. During the first five years of ownership, a new car value depreciates between 15 and 25 percent every year. Therefore, buying new is a terrible idea because the value of your purchase drops significantly during the first part of its useful life. Check out the rapid decline in value on the BMW purchase in the following chart.

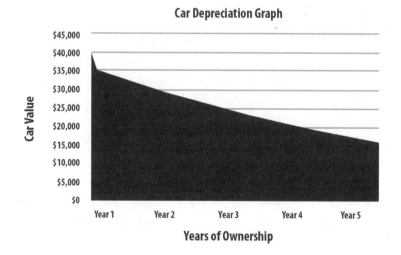

If you are going to buy a car, then buy used. The sweet spot for purchasing used cars is when depreciation plateaus, around year 4 or 5. If you buy in this time frame, the car will have all of the latest features, but you can escape the wrath of the early depreciation curve.

Not all cars depreciate at the same rate. Some brands hold their value much longer than others, so do your research and check out websites like Edmunds.com or ConsumerReports.org to compare depreciation rates on cars you are considering.

2. Don't Lease

At first glance, leasing a new car can seem like an enticing idea. You get to drive the newest cars, forgo the capital expenditure of purchasing, and often receive the option to buy the car at the end of the lease.

Don't fall for it.

According to ConsumerReports.org, "The financial workings of leasing are so confusing that people don't realize that leasing invariably costs more than an equivalent loan. And even if they did, the extra cost is difficult to calculate."[9]

There are often hidden fees that dramatically increase the cost of leasing: finance charges, mileage overage charges, or high down payments. The probability of getting a great deal on leasing a car is extremely low. Leasing a car almost always benefits the car dealership. Leasing allows the dealership to move inventory and make money on financing.

Don't confuse short-term affordability with sound financial management. Listen to the professionals who have already run the numbers and are telling you to avoid the leasing trap. Avoid locking yourself into fixed monthly payments because it is financially stifling. While you are in the money makeover, your goal is to free up as much of your monthly cash flow as possible.

3. Think Long Term

Buying a car is one of the largest purchases that you will make as a young professional, so it is important to do it right. Be strategic and think about the long-term nature of your purchase.

Although flashy cars are alluring, buy something that is realistic. The sexy brands typically lack utility and practicality—two of the most important factors when car shopping. The rich have made this a rule for themselves.

Research conducted by *Experian Automotive* showed that 61 percent of people who earned more than $250,000 per year do not buy luxury brand cars (think Mercedes, Lexus, BMW). It turns out that the rich buy Fords, Toyotas, and Hondas.[10] They aim for dependability, longevity, and affordability. You should too.

4. Calculate the Total Cost of Ownership (TCO)

The sticker price is simply the beginning of the cost calculation. Unfortunately, most people (not you) only consider the purchase price when determining affordability.

The problem with this approach is that there are tons of hidden, related, and invisible costs that purchasers fail to take into account. If you don't consider these costs when calculating affordability, they can weigh you down later.

Here is a list of variables to consider when calculating the TCO:

- Initial purchase price
- Tax and tag fees
- Car insurance

- Gas or electricity
- Repair and maintenance fees
- Warranties
- Resale value
- Length of ownership

Calculating the TCO will give you the most accurate comparison when deciding between cars. Once you have factored in all of the variables, don't let emotions get the better of you. Choose wisely.

5. Pay With Cash

You might have picked up on a theme throughout the money makeover: You should eliminate debt. This applies to all forms of debt, including consumer debt. If you have found the car that you want to buy, then save up the cash to purchase it.

This is an old-school approach to a new-school problem.

Millennials are highly leveraged. To shift from the affordability mindset to the ownership mindset, you must view things as how much they are going to cost you in *cold hard cash*. By making your purchases this way, you are ratcheting up the full pain of the transaction. Otherwise, by financing your car purchase, the pain is very small up front, but evenly deferred to each car payment. Why opt for death by a thousand cuts?

Paying for your car in cash will help you in three ways: It reduces your ability to purchase beyond your means; it keeps you out of debt; and it allows you to negotiate the best deal possible.

....

MILLENNIAL MONEY MAKEOVER PRINCIPLE OF SUCCESS: DEBT IS NOT A NECESSARY EVIL

You make hundreds of transactions throughout the month, from grabbing drinks with friends to purchasing furniture for your apartment. How you purchase large and small items matters. Avoid financing at all costs.

....

6. Negotiate

When you have found the car you want and have saved up the necessary cash, it is time to start negotiating. Let the dance begin.

Some of the best deals are won through the art of negotiation. This dance between buyer and seller involves both parties trying to discern what the other party truly wants. Here are some questions to ask yourself during this process:

- Why is the owner selling the car?
- Are you the first person to see the car?
- How long has the car been on the market?
- Are you prepared to walk away from the deal?

Because you have cash in hand, you hold the ace card. Your cash ceiling allows you to work with the seller and provides you a stopping criterion.

Above all, when you are looking to buy your first car be diligent in your research and check your emotions. Determine the car you want, pay with cash, and negotiate the best deal possible. You will learn countless lessons along the way.

Large-Ticket Purchase 2: Love and Money

Millennials want more out of life.

This generational craving has led to a focus on the self and the decision to delay life's major milestones, such as engagement, marriage, and family. Throughout the past three decades, the average age of marriage has skyrocketed to twenty-seven years old for women and twenty-nine years old for men.[11] But looking at the numbers tells only half the story.

The postponement of life's milestones also happens to coincide with Millennials' lack of earning power and financial health. Now more than ever it is important for Millennials to be cautious when mixing love and money.

This means your relationship health is dependent upon having difficult conversations with your partner about love, money, debt, your future, and family planning. You need to have what I call the "define the financial relationship" (DTFR) talk. This conversation might feel a little awkward, but discussing your financial reality early on will help you work out kinks in your relationship and determine whether the relationship is a good match.

How you have this conversation is just as important as *having* the conversation. I suggest getting a bottle of wine, dedicating some time on the calendar, and sitting down to have this intimate financial discussion. Both of you will be nervous. Have faith that it will go well.

Erin Lowry, author of *Broke Millennial*, says getting financially naked is a fundamental relationship step to have with your partner. Getting financially naked involves defining how much debt you have, going over your credit reports and scores, and how you are currently handling your debt.

Lowry adds, "This doesn't mean you have to pull up all your bank statements, credit card bills, student loan payments, and investments during the first talk, but it's imperative that you both disclose approximate numbers, positive or negative, when the time is right."[12]

Mixing love and money can be potent to your pocketbook. It is crucial to make your expectations clear, be honest, and create an open rapport with your partner. After all, this is only the beginning.

Five Questions to Ask Your Significant Other

Divorce rates are high, and one of the leading contributors to divorce is a money problem.[13] However, money problems can be solved early. Just like conversations about careers, children, or where you want to live, being open about money will help you determine if your partner is the right fit and whether you both want the same things out of life.

Having the DTFR conversation early in your relationship will only strengthen it. If you are thinking about getting engaged, married, or moving in together, consider asking your significant other these five questions:

1. How Much Do You Have in Savings?

Savings is paramount to financial health. According to a 2015 Google Consumer Survey, 62 percent of Americans have less than $1,000 in their savings account.[14] Are you one of these people? Is your partner one? Do either of you have a savings plan?

The chances are that one of you will have more saved than the other. "It's almost impossible to be hooked up to somebody who has the same balance of spender and saver as you, or expansiveness versus conservativeness or financial circumstances," says psychologist Gregory A. Kuhlman.[15]

It is important to find out which one of you is the spender and which one is the saver. So which one are you? Are you both financial mavens with thousands stored away? Or are you both broke? Either way, knowing your savings cushion gives true insight into your current financial outlook and can set the tone for the rest of the conversation. Beginning your financial conversation with savings can provide tremendous insights into your partner's financial health.

2. Do You Have a Plan for Getting Out of Debt?

Statistically speaking, both of you are in debt. But the kind of debt—student loans, credit card, or consumer debt—matters. Each of these debts carries with it a different story. Knowing the good, the bad, and the ugly will give you a glimpse into the future.

As you learned earlier, the average college graduate will have thousands of dollars in student loans. If you both fall into this category, then knowing that your partner is also dealing with this stress can be both a liberating and bonding experience.

Maybe you both had to pay for college or graduate school. Perhaps one of you got lucky and your parents paid for your education. Whatever the case, discussing your financial reality can provide needed insights into financial behaviors.

A typical red flag will be your partner's credit card debt. This can be a sign of poor financial planning, shopping gone wild, trying to keep up with the Joneses, or a more systemic spending issue. Let's face it: We all have our weaknesses, such as a spa day, a new suit, eating out, or happy hours. Sometimes it is just hard to say no. Discussing credit cards provides a peek into each other's outlook on consumerism.

3. Have You Started Saving for Retirement?

If you are serious about your partner, then you probably want to be with him or her for a long time. And if you plan on getting engaged or married, then your commitment to each other is forever. So, why not start planning now?

Forming an idea of what you want your life to look like together thirty years from now will help fortify your relationship, while at the same time establish clear expectations for the future. Saving for retirement is one of those things, which if done early enough, can be a nonissue later in life. If you find that you are both slightly behind on saving for retirement, don't worry. We will discuss more of this in Chapter 5.

4. What Is Your Ideal Income?

In the movie *Wall Street: Money Never Sleeps,* the main character, Jacob Moore, asks the banking titan Bretton James, "What is your number?" Cool, calm, and with a wry smile, James answers, "More."[16]

How much money do you want to make? How much does your partner want to make? Does that comingle with your discussion on career and family?

If your fiancée wants to be a partner at a law firm because she worked her butt off in law school, are you okay with that lifestyle? Will one of you work and the other care for children? Does one of you value making partner while the other is content not chasing after the corner office?

If you have an ideal income to attain, chasing after your goal can give you the necessary motivation to fuel your path to success. The question forces you both, as a couple, to start thinking about where you are in life and where you want to go.

5. Can You Be Poor With Me?

Fortunes are gained and lost every day. Relying on money to fuel a relationship is an uphill battle. Money is simply a means of providing texture to your life story. Your story will contain twists and turns, and being prepared for these changes will be just as important as navigating them together. Making sure you are both comfortable with little money is a testament to the strength of your relationship. Even if only for a short time, it is worth conducting an experiment and living on the "cheapest fare." The results will be eye-opening.

> *"Set aside a certain number of days, during which you shall be content with the scantiest and cheapest fare, with coarse and rough dress, saying to yourself all the while: Is this the condition that I feared?"*
> —Seneca[17]

Open and honest conversations about personal finances can help resolve significant issues early that would otherwise cause problems later down the road. Remove the financial facade and get financially naked. Have the DTFR talk now and save yourself time, energy, and money.

On Buying the Ring

Okay, so you had the DTFR talk. If your relationship survives that conversation, you can now enter into a world of continued open and honest financial rapport. Knowing how much each of you has saved, if you are in debt, your retirement goals, your ideal incomes, and your willingness to get through the tough times is a priceless relationship asset, albeit intangible.

If you are still head over heels, then congratulations. But it's time to get real and not let the love goggles cloud your financial intelligence. The next step is finding and saving for a ring. Are you ready? No, are you *really* ready?

Buying an engagement ring is usually where the financial train derails. Common sense goes out the door, emotions are at an all-time high, and egos are at stake.

Conventional wisdom tells us that if we *love* our significant other, then the ring needs to be big and expensive, symbolic of our love. This has led to the cultural maxim that you should spend two to three months of salary on an engagement ring.

I call *bullshit* and here is why.

Economic researchers Andrew Francis and Hugo Mialon of Emory University set out to find the correlation between how much people spent on weddings and divorce rates.[18] What they found surprised a lot of people and challenged conventional wisdom. As it turns out, a diamond is *not* forever.

In a survey of more than 3,000 "ever-married persons in the United States," Francis and Mialon discovered that divorce rates and the size of the engagement ring were directly correlated. Their findings revealed an inverse relationship between how much people spent on engagement rings and whether that couple stood the test of time. You read that correctly. The more you spend on the engagement ring, the more likely you are to have your marriage end in divorce.

Their findings run counter to cultural standards, and that is by design. If you feel the pressure to buy expensive engagement rings, you can thank Gernold Lauck of the N.W. Ayer advertising agency. In 1938, De Beers, the world-renowned diamond company, turned to Lauck for marketing advice. Lauck commissioned a study to help De Beers market to young professional men—their ideal target customers. He pitched that it was critical to link the diamond to love. The core message needed to be that the larger and finer the diamond, the greater the expression of love.[19] De Beers began preaching this as gospel, and the accretive effect has altered the diamond industry.

In an attempt to raise revenues even more, a well-designed marketing campaign by De Beers in the 1980s sought to increase the standard on how much men spent on engagement rings. De Beers created a slogan that was rather catchy: "Isn't two months' salary a small price to pay for something that lasts forever?"[20]

As time went on, this campaign sunk deeper and deeper into the consumer psyche, and during the economic booms of the 1980s and 1990s, the corporate slogan took a firm hold on consumer behavior.

However, during the economic collapse of 2008, millions of families started to halt their purchases on large-ticket items. For struggling Millennials, buying large engagement rings was simply a nonstarter. Would-be purchasers also realized that a diamond is a terrible investment. Diamonds can depreciate by as much as 50 percent as soon as you walk out of the store.[21] From an investment perspective, it doesn't get much worse than that.

When you are in the market for an engagement ring, keep this thought in mind: The size of the diamond does not correlate to your love. Hopefully, after having the DTFR talk, your partner will be on the same page as you.

A word of caution: If you have skipped ahead in this book and still have debt of any kind, you should not, under any circumstances, think that spending thousands of dollars on an engagement ring is justifiable. If you have debt, eliminate it completely and *then* save up enough cash to purchase the engagement ring. As a newly engaged couple, there will be plenty of expenses coming your way. Be strategic and thoughtful about this process. You will thank yourself later for your discipline today.

How to 10X Your Wedding

A wedding is a big event. Once you know your wedding budget, you will want to optimize every allocated dollar to having the wedding you deserve. The wedding industry is about to welcome you with open arms.

Throughout the last several decades, the wedding industry has experienced unprecedented growth, as there has been a major push to "commodify love and romance."[22] According to TheKnot.com, in 2015 the average wedding cost $32,641.[23] I hope you have been saving.

Planning for a wedding means that you are going to have to be a master at juggling seating arrangements, ordering food, coordinating with the band, and organizing flower deliveries, just to name a few. The options about what you want to have in your wedding can seem endless, so it is important to focus on exactly what you want and not get distracted by all of the noise. Don't get caught in the vortex of the paradox of choice.

You can 10X your wedding experience by placing your "must haves" at the top of your priority list. Concentrate on making sure those are done well. Then, as The Beatles say, "Let it be." Here are three ways to maximize the impact of your wedding budget:

1. Share Your Budget

The wedding industry is ripe with revenue. That means that there are wedding experts to handle all different tiers of weddings, no matter the budget. There are wedding planners who specialize in the $100,000 wedding. And the $50,000 wedding. And the $10,000 wedding. And the $3,000 wedding too.

The first step is for you to determine your budget. Once you know how much you can spend, it is time to start looking for vendors that align with that number. Weddings happen every day. Wedding planners, caters, or virtually anyone accepting a check will see your "special day" as business as usual. So treat it as such.

When you are negotiating with vendors, share your budget with them. Honesty is the best policy. You want to get an excellent bang for your buck, and vendors want to give you the best of what they can offer. Plus, they will be relieved by your transparency.

See how far they are willing to stretch your dollar. If you like them, great. If not, move on to the next vendor. Light a fire in your negotiations by getting counterbids. There is nothing businesses hate more than losing revenue, and losing that revenue to the competition is even worse. See how badly they want your business.

2. Look for Discounts and the Rising Stars

There is an old saying, "If you don't ask, you will never know." Once you have selected your preferred vendor, ask if they provide discounts.

Put them in the hot seat. Do they offer volume discounts? What about a Sunday wedding? Another tactic is to look for the rising star in your city. The wedding industry is awash with talent. This means newcomers are always trying to make a name for themselves. These rising starts will usually give you better deals and work longer and harder than their more seasoned competition. Find the people who are willing to put in the extra hours to ensure that your special day is everything you want. These are the people you want on your team.

3. Leverage Your Wedding Registry

A wedding is a celebration of two people becoming one. Commercially, this is displayed on your wedding registry. Luckily, technology has made this easier for the couple and the guests with the advent of the online wedding registry.

Use this to your advantage by being thoughtful and strategic with your listing. Here are a couple of points to keep in mind while you are working on your registry.

- *Be selective.* Aiming for quality over quantity is a great way to make sure your registry stands the test of time. Resist the urge to be extravagant. Be fair to your guests when you are selecting items to put on your registry.

- *View it as a money saver.* The wedding registry process is a chance to eliminate your basic needs. Decorating a living room, bedroom, or kitchen requires more effort than meets the eye. Take this opportunity to get the basics out of the way.

- *Register at a few places only.* The paradox of choice is real. By giving your guests only a few places to shop, being selective, and choosing quality items, the likelihood that you will receive everything you want increases dramatically.

- *Set up your registry early.* With the average couple enjoying a fifteen-month engagement, there is plenty of time to plan.[24] Take an inventory of what you and your future spouse separately own. Be prepared to discuss exactly what additional items you will need to purchase once you consolidate assets. This will alleviate paying for duplicate items, and you can start putting money toward a honeymoon, savings, or investments.

Although your wedding is a personal statement, it is also a moment for reflection, family, and fun. Don't let the commodifying effect of your special day steal your happiness or attention away from what matters. Above all else, enjoying your wedding day with your new spouse is the best way to maximize your wedding.

Large-Ticket Purchase 3: Buying a House

Peter Thiel is one of Silicon Valley's household names. As a cofounder of PayPal, Thiel made a name for himself when he sold his once fledgling business for $11 billion in 2002. The mystique around Thiel and his ragtag group of cofounders, dubbed the "PayPal Mafia," has only grown with time.

Now an established player in Silicon Valley, Thiel is known for his contrarian views on business. In his bestselling book *Zero to One,* Thiel makes the argument that competition is bad for business. Instead, as a founder, you want to look for monopolies.[25] This is not an everyday American viewpoint.

One of Thiel's most well-known attributes is the unique way he conducts interviews. As the founder of multiple companies, Thiel understands the importance people play in building a successful business and is no stranger to interviewing executives.

In fact, his interview questions have only increased his lore. One of his most famous questions is, "Can you tell me something that is true that no one agrees with?"

If Thiel asked me that question, I would have an answer: I believe buying a house is one of the worst financial decisions young professionals can make.

Buying a house is not inherently a bad investment, but buying a house *too early in life* is often one of the biggest financial mistakes someone can make, and it has years of lasting consequences. The fascination of purchasing the *perfect* home in a *great* neighborhood transcends the rational reality of financial wisdom. What follows is a focus on the affordability of mortgage payments in lieu of creating a proper financial base to secure your financial future.

Homeownership is deeply embedded in American culture, but a systemic issue with housing is that people get sucked into the idea that they need to purchase too much house. This leaves them financially riddled with high mortgage payments. In an economy where the average Millennial changes jobs every 3.7 years[26] and the typical American moves 11.4 times in their life,[27] the utility of buying a house is not what it used to be.

The money makeover has one major rule on housing: Do not buy a house until you have accumulated at least one to two times your annual household income in cash or investments.

Pundits will hate this. Banks will brush this aside. Realtors will laugh in your face. Ignore them all because the traditional view of housing is outdated.

The reality is that this rule gives you the financial momentum to combat the temptation of purchasing a house that will break your budget, cause high anxiety, buyer's remorse, ballooning mortgage payments, and low cash reserves. This rule offers a hedge against your innate inability to process large numbers and tendency to bite off more than you can chew. This rule flips the traditional order of the success sequence and emphasizes securing your financial future first.

With soaring real estate prices, the affordability of housing has plummeted throughout the last several decades. Yet the pressure to purchase still remains high. Millennials are left caught in this paradox. The *dream* of homeownership needs to be reevaluated because it can quickly morph into a financial *nightmare.*

Here are the four most common mistakes that young homebuyers make.

1. Buying Too Soon

It pays to be prepared. Buying a house before you are financially secure is the biggest mistake you can make. Many homebuyers are lured into the pressure of homeownership by external factors, such as nagging family and friends or keeping pace with marketed societal norms. Before buying a home, I advise having more important aspects of your financial life fully secured.

2. Having Other Debts

Before buying a home, you should have completed Step 2 of the money makeover. That means you should have no student loans, credit card debt, or consumer debt. Get rid of all your debt before you even *think* about buying a house.

Practically speaking, all of your expenses will go up once you purchase a house. You will have to furnish the house, pay real estate taxes, buy home insurance, pay broker fees, incur repair and maintenance costs and countless other unforeseen expenses. All of these hidden costs of homeownership are not included in the sticker price, only furthering the total cost of purchase.

3. Not Saving One to Two Times
Their Household Income

This can be in investments, retirement savings, or cold hard cash, but first-time homeowners often forego securing a healthy financial base before buying a home. This financial foundation will provide you the support you need to establish a healthy ecosystem. The momentum of this savings base will carry you to a rich future. As you saw earlier, humans' ability to conceptualize large numbers is pretty poor. Don't let the numbers work against you on such a monumental purchase.

If you are researching buying a home, then you should already have at least one to two times your annual household income saved before taking the plunge into homeownership. This will dampen your desire to purchase beyond your means because this savings base will act as a relative and tangible point of comparison.

4. Not Putting 20 Percent Down

One of the most prohibitive aspects of purchasing a home is the down payment. This is meant to be a gatekeeper. The down payment was designed as a barrier to entry because it prevents purchasers from buying houses they cannot afford.

Millennials are no strangers to the financial difficulty of homeownership, and major tech companies in the housing space are paying attention. "Young workers face a lot of hurdles on the way to homeownership, including saving for a down payment in the first place and deciding where and when to settle down," said Zillow's chief economist, Stena Gudell.[28]

Saving for a down payment can take years, but it doesn't have to be painful. Set up a savings account and automate 5 to 10 percent of your income to automatically pile up in this account (see Chapter 6). Then put these savings on cruise control until you are ready to purchase.

When done correctly, homeownership can be a financial blessing. But it does not make sense for everyone. Evaluate where you are on your money makeover before taking the plunge.

Interest Distorts Your View, Again

In this section, we will analyze the nature of interest and its inherent ability to increase the total cost of purchase of a mortgage. We will look at two very different home purchasers, Tom and Susan, and the financial repercussions of their choices when purchasing a home. For the sake of this demonstration, we are going to assume the perspective homeowners will pay the average purchase price of a first home in 2016, or $362,000.[29]

Scenario 1

Tom is an information technology manager. He makes good money working for a startup, where he has been employed for the last two years. The good news is that Tom enjoys his job. However, Tom took out massive student loans to afford his high-tech education. Recently, Tom and his wife started exploring the idea of owning a home. As the parents of a two-year-old, they found out recently that there would soon be another member of the family, turning their manageable apartment for three into close quarters for a family of four.

Tom starts to analyze the pros and cons of buying a house, even though he knows he should pay off his debt first. Going against the money makeover, Tom decides to defer his student loan payments and save for a down payment of 5 percent. He purchases the house with a thirty-year fixed loan with an interest rate of only 4.591 percent. Not bad—he thinks.

Tom's $362,000 house will cost him $652,110 over the life of his loan. This includes the $343,900 of principal payments and the whopping $290,110 of interest payments.

Scenario 2

Sarah is a lawyer. And a damn good one. During her first couple years out of law school, she made a name for herself in her private practice. However, don't let her high income deceive you. Sarah is up to her neck in debt. But Sarah and her husband are adamant about paying it off quickly, even with small children.

Crammed in a two-bedroom apartment, Sarah feels like her income doesn't translate to her lifestyle. Sarah wants to buy a house to give the family more space. Plus, all of Sarah's friends have upgraded to purchasing homes. She feels pressure from her family and friends to make the plunge into homeownership. But Sarah has read *Millennial Money Makeover*, and she knows that she still has debt to eliminate.

After hunkering down and getting rid of all of their debt, Sarah and her husband then save one times their household income, which took significant delayed gratification. Next, Sarah and her husband concentrate on saving for a down payment. Within eighteen months, they have enough to put down 20 percent on a $362,000 house.

Sarah's finances are in order. Because she is financially secure with no debt and a 20 percent down payment, Sarah decides to opt for a fifteen-year fixed loan with an interest rate of only 3.645 percent. Not bad—she knows.

Sarah's $362,000 house will cost her $448,777 over the life of her loan. This includes the $289,600 of principal payments and $86,777 of interest payments.

Total Cost of First House Purchase			
Variables	Tom	Sarah	Variance
Home cost	$362,000	$362,000	$0
Interest rate	4.591%	3.645%	0.946%
Length of loan	30 years	15 years	15 years
Down payment	$18,100	$72,400	$54,300
Total principal	$343,900	$289,600	$54,300
Total interest	$290,110	$86,777	$203,333
Total cost	$652,110	$448,777	$203,333
*Data provided by Zillow Mortgage Calculator			

The total cost difference over the life of the loans is a whopping $203,333.[30]

Or roughly four times the average American household income.[31]

Or more than double the average 401(k) balance in 2016.[32]

The gaping difference between the cost of the same home, based upon the length of mortgage and size of the down payment, is why we are concentrating on housing now and are not leaving it as an aside in a later chapter. Decisions on housing can financially make or break you.

MILLENNIAL MONEY MAKEOVER PRINCIPLE OF SUCCESS: LEARNING FROM EXPERIENCE IS TOO SLOW

Getting large purchases right will save you thousands of dollars throughout the course of your life. Leverage the experience of those who have gone before you and make rich decisions.

Five Reasons Millennials Aren't Buying Homeownership

Homeownership is a hallmark of the American dream. With average new home sales now topping $380,000, the dream of homeownership has become daunting for Millennials.[33] The idea of becoming a first-time homeowner seems to be more of an illusion than a pillar of the American experience.

Millennials are shifting the tide on the timing of traditional life-stage purchases, and many don't view buying a house as a necessary reality, as once advertised by previous generations.[33] The weight of costly student loans, consumer debt, and recent urbanization has transformed the Millennial outlook away from traditional homeownership. Housing trends among Millennials are changing the norm. Here are five reasons Millennials aren't subscribing to the traditional mantra of first-time homeownership.

1. New Housing Isn't for Millennials

Despite the headlines about the surging housing market, people in their twenties and thirties don't feel they can participate in the boom. There is a disconnect between what Millennials read in the news and what they are experiencing in reality. Surveys conducted by the National Home Owners Association show that less than 20 percent of the new home construction over the past several years was dedicated to "entry-level" properties.[34] This is down from the pre-recession levels of more than 30 percent. In short, houses are literally not being built for the Millennial market.

Instead, developers have shifted their focus to building larger houses that cater directly to the more established and affluent Baby Boomers. Until there is a shift back to building affordable first-time homes, this trend is likely to continue.[35]

2. Down Payments Are the Worst

If the average sales price for new homes stands around $380,000, with some quick math, you can see that the average Millennial needs to amass $76,000 for the recommended 20 percent down payment for the average house.[36] However, Millennials clearly face major financial burdens that restrict their ability to accumulate the necessary down payment to make purchasing a house a viable option.

To complicate matters, most Millennials tend to live in large urban areas where housing prices are higher than the national average. Thus, the practicality of buying a house is quickly dismissed.

Some Millennials are taking a nontraditional approach to saving for a down payment and living at home longer. According to *Forbes,* for the first time in more than 130 years, more Millennials are living with their parents than with a significant other.[37] For the few Millennials who are buying houses, their time at home serves as a strategic move to allow them to save enough cash to afford their down payment.

3. Flexibility Is More Valuable

With major cultural shifts occurring, many Millennials don't feel the need to be strapped down by purchasing a first-time home. Not only are Millennials pushing "adulting" to later in life, they honestly don't quite see the need for the mortgage and the white picket fence. Thanks to personal finance advocates, a home mortgage is now viewed as a liability and not the asset it was once considered.

In today's fluid economy, Millennials value flexibility and mobility over security and stability. Therefore, the pressure to find a house and settle down to long-term employment isn't what it used to be. Millennials are privately thankful for that because, honestly, they can't afford it.

4. Rental Options Are Abundant

Although Millennials are not warming up to the new housing market, they are doing quite well in subscribing to the renter's market. Even as rents rise, urban-based Millennials are left with the option of finding an "affordable" place to rent. In fact, the cost of renting is rising faster than inflation. This leaves Millennials paying a larger percentage of their take-home income on housing.[38]

Although rents remain high, they are not high enough to incentivize saving for a down payment and often impede the progress toward saving for that goal. Additionally, after watching families struggle following the housing collapse of 2008, many believe homeownership is not worth the risk. And if renting an apartment doesn't work, there is always Mom and Dad's house (see Reason 2).

5. It's the Economy, Stupid

As with most generations, Millennials' outlook and consumption patterns are often driven by the economic conditions of their time. Many Millennials graduated from college or were exposed to the job market during the economic collapse of 2008 and felt its lasting ramifications. Over the last decade, salaries have been relatively stagnant and economic growth anemic. As a result of this slow growth, Millennials have focused on staying solvent and financially afloat. Until the economy fully turns around, Millennials will be patient, waiting their turn.

The takeaway is that purchasing a home, if done *incorrectly*, can be a giant mistake. Even in the wake of the housing crisis of the last decade, people are still not abiding by the rational mantra that homeownership has its time and place in life's milestones. Don't let other people's ideas of what your future should look like define yours. Learning to be patient with large purchases, especially housing, can be the quickest path to the rich life.

Thoughts on Financial Leverage

Semantics matter.

When it comes to buying large-ticket items, people often confuse affordability with ownership. The ability to *make* monthly payments on a new car, boat, or house does not justify the purchase. Affordability is not a synonym for ownership.

Although you might be able to make the payments, this does not mean that you *should*. The ability to meet the minimum monthly payments blinds people to the true questions they should be asking:

- Does this purchase make financial sense?
- Does it align with my goals?
- Will this purchase wreak havoc on my budget?
- Is this a rich decision?

The only major purchase you should finance is your house. All other purchases should be made with cash.

In fitness, the Body Mass Index gives a quick glimpse into physical health. The financial equivalent is called the financial leverage ratio.

Typical Household Items	
Assets	**Liabilities**
Cash	Credit card debt
Investments	Student loans
Furniture	Car note
Jewelry/Electronics	Mortgage

Financial Leverage = Household Liabilities/Household Assets

This ratio provides a gauge of financial health. The higher your financial leverage ratio, the more debts your household carries relative to its assets. A high financial leverage ratio can foreshadow financial disaster. One missed payment, one emergency, or one layoff could derail everything.

Conversely, a low financial leverage ratio indicates a stronger financial makeup. Ideally, you want this ratio to hover around zero. And once you complete all of the steps in Chapter 2, and are completely debt free, your goal will be to keep this as low as possible. Financing large purchases can skyrocket this ratio, especially for young working professionals. If you graduated from college with the typical debt load, you probably haven't had the time to increase your household assets. Since you have debt and relatively few assets, you are *highly* leveraged. Due to interest on your loans, your liabilities will continue to grow. This is why in Chapter 2 you worked to eliminate your debts as quickly as possible.

Once you have eliminated your debt, your financial ratio will start looking much healthier, and you can start building up your assets (cash, bonds, stocks, real estate, and so on). Keep tabs on this ratio and don't overexpose yourself to debt. If you follow the money makeover principles to success you will protect yourself from being overexposed.

Action Items

Applying the lessons learned in this chapter will accelerate your money makeover. They will work like magic. You might not see all of the benefits immediately, but the results will pay for themselves in perpetuity. Your bank account with be healthier, your life will be richer, and you will find happiness in your decisions.

When you are making large milestone purchases, remember the following ideas from this chapter:

1. Buying a new car is for suckers; do your research.

2. Mixing love and money can be dangerous; proceed with caution.

3. Buying a house should only be done when you are financial prepared.

4. Remember that education does not end in the classroom.

5. Optimize large purchases and expedite your makeover.

Optimizing large purchases will propel you into the rich life. Being smart with your money is not always the easiest path. But this discipline will open your eyes to the reality that life is about more than material possessions. Remaining financially secure and making measured financial choices is a cornerstone of your money makeover.

This decision will allow you the mental space to begin preparing for accumulating investments and saving for the future. The rich life is about forward thinking. In the next chapter, you will learn how to turn your financial diligence into a wealth-generating machine.

Let's start the engine.

5

....

MINTING MOMENTUM: SAVING, INVESTING, AND CONSTRUCTING YOUR RETIREMENT

*Wealth that stayeth to give enjoyment and satisfaction
to its owner comes gradually, because it is a child born
of knowledge and persistent purpose.*
—George Claşon, *The Richest Man in Babylon*

If you are an average Millennial, saving for the future has not been a top priority. However, if you have read this far, you already accomplished what most never will. You have turned professional with your money. You have paid off your debts. Your budget is humming on autopilot. You are optimizing all your large purchases. Now it is time for the fun part: getting rich.

Building wealth is a habit. In this chapter, you will learn how to reinforce that habit by building an emergency fund and reaching slush-fund status, as well as learn to invest and save for retirement.

The rich life is quickly approaching. Now is the perfect time to welcome it with open arms and lay a remarkable foundation.

MILLENNIAL MONEY MAKEOVER

Humans Aren't Wired for Saving

The state of Millennial savings needs a drastic makeover.

Most Millennials simply have not saved enough cash for unexpected expenses, true emergencies, or retirement. It seems the more conceptual the event, the more ill-equipped Millennials are to save. According to the Federal Reserve's 2013 Survey of Consumer Finances by economists from the Economic Policy Institute, "Nearly half of working-age families have nothing saved in retirement accounts, and the median working-age family had only $5,000 saved in 2013."[1]

Clearly, we have some work to do.

This chapter is about answering a fundamental question: Arc you saving enough? Depending on where you are in life, it is one of those questions that can elicit extraordinarily different responses. The answers typically go something like this:

- *Twentysomething:* Saving? Isn't that something only wealthy people do? I plan on saving more in the future, but right now I am just trying to survive.

- *Thirtysomething:* Saving? Well, I have a 401(k). Does that count? I would save more, but my kids and house are much more expensive than I anticipated!

- *Fortysomething:* Saving? Of course I am saving. But have you seen college tuition recently? My financial advisor tells me it is going to cost me a quarter of a million dollars to send my kids to college!

- *Fiftysomething:* Saving? I can tell you one thing: Working every day is getting old. I feel like I need to start putting more money toward retirement so that it will finally get there someday.

The data is clear; most people are not living the money makeover lifestyle. As a result, their approach to savings is haphazard, and this leads to dangerously low savings. But how have these abysmal savings habits come to pass? How has the "Do It Yourself" retirement system failed so many people? One reason could be that humans aren't wired for saving.

Like any machine or software, we are only as good as our operating system. One part of our developed brains, which makes us uniquely human and sets us apart from other animals, is our frontal lobe. This more recent evolutionary development allows humans to imagine the future and develop a more robust understanding of the world. Our frontal lobe gives us the capacity to plan for the future, which can be wonderfully advantageous. However, it can also produce anxiety surrounding the anticipation of how that future will unfold.

From a financial perspective, modern man relies on the frontal lobe to see the need to save for retirement. It turns out, with all of the frontal lobe's amazing benefits, it does have some faults. When we think about deferring savings, we tend to enjoy the thought of reaching the savings goal more than actually doing the saving.

Humans enjoy visualizing the completed product. As Harvard psychology professor Daniel Gilbert emphasizes in his book *Stumbling on Happiness,* one problem with dreaming into the future is, "people find it easy to imagine an event, and they overestimate the likelihood that it will actually occur."[2] In other words, there is a gap between where we are *now* and the *future* we imagine. Our imagination bridges that disconnect. That imaginary bridge holds us back from actually saving as much as we should, unless we convert the imaginary into tangible and actionable steps. This process is critical to long-term financial success and overriding our core operating system.

Another caveat with the frontal lobe is how it works. Although we can imagine ourselves in the future, we default to imagining the *current version* of ourselves. When it comes to successfully saving, the *version* of ourselves we see in the future can have a profound effect on how we save.

To demonstrate this, Hall Hershfield, a social psychologist at New York University, conducted an experiment. Participants were asked to wear virtual reality headsets, and Hall divided the participants into two groups. The first group saw a digital representation of themselves in their current state for a brief time span. The second group also saw a visual representation of themselves, but this time, a software program aged the participants' images to seventy years old. After using the virtual reality headset, both groups of participants were asked a series of questions. One of the questions regarded money allocation: What would you do with $1,000?

The group who saw themselves at their current age said they would save $80 for retirement. The group who saw the older version of themselves allocated $173—more than *twice* the first group—for retirement.[3]

According to the researchers, thinking about yourself in the future as your current version is equivalent to thinking about a stranger (no wonder you only gave up $80).[4] But when you harness the power of technology and virtually age yourself, the stranger becomes much more familiar. The stranger becomes, well, you. This visualization process can have a tremendous impact on how much you save during the course of your life.

When we are reminded that growing old will happen whether we like it or not, an internal change takes place.

Visualizing the aged version of yourself can be the difference between saving 8 percent or 16 percent for retirement. Throughout the course of a career, that can produce 401(k) millionaires (more on this shortly).

Savings Makes You Look Younger

"Not only do I feel better, but I just don't have to worry about things as much," said one of my blog readers. The positive psychological benefits of having a financial buffer are amazing. Your outlook on life becomes positive and forward-thinking because you don't worry about meeting the present.

The mind is a wonderfully complex machine, and when it knows that it has room to breathe, it thanks the body. Knowing that losing your job, damaging a car, or paying an unexpected medical bill won't leave you broke can create space in your life. This space can be used to concentrate on other tasks. Instead of slogging through the day-to-day struggle, you can focus on doing things you enjoy and start looking younger during the process.

Stress ages people, and financial stress is no exception. A recent study on financial stress showed that worrying about money can make you appear older. According to Margie Lachman, a psychology professor at Brandeis University and one of the study's authors, surprised researchers discovered, "financial stress was related just to how old you looked to others. It was not related to how old one feels or how old one thinks they look. So it showed up to others in one's appearance, but not in terms of one's own subjective views or perceptions of their age."[5]

Researchers speculated as to why participants would appear older to others when they were financially stressed, but the question is still unanswered.

Perhaps people who don't have to worry about money can:

- Spend more time working out
- Take the time to care for their appearance
- Afford more nutritional meals and snacks
- Buy higher-quality clothing and beauty products
- Spend less time frowning

The point is: Erasing financial stress can have a massively positive impact on your life. By removing the weight of poor finances, you can distance yourself from the paycheck-to-paycheck lifestyle. This allows you to do more of the things you love. Let's learn how to create that space in a specific sequence, which begins with building up a cash cushion and ends with FU money.

How to Reach FU Status

Financial peace of mind equals cash accumulation. But the vast majority of people just don't have enough cash saved. Paying off reoccurring debt, trying to strike it rich with the next hot investment, or spending on the sparkle of a new purchase distracts even seasoned finance aficionados from savings. The following steps are critical to generating enough savings to eliminate financial stress and begin looking younger immediately.

Step 1. Start an Emergency Fund

Virtually every financial advisor (human or machine) has one rule: Make sure you have an emergency fund. This is especially true for people who are starting to get their finances together for the first time. An emergency cushion, as it is so aptly named, is a preventative measure to stop you from dipping into your savings in the event of unforeseen unemployment, unexpected medical bills, or a random accident.

For those who don't have savings set aside for emergencies, there is a temptation to pay for unexpected bills with credit. This can begin, or even perpetuate, a credit card debt cycle. The financially fit prepare for the inevitable emergency.

Personal finance personalities such as Dave Ramsey and Clark Howard popularized the concept of the emergency fund. On Ramsey's award-winning talk radio show, *The Dave Ramsey Show*, he argues that you should have at least $1,000 set aside in your emergency fund. And he was right—twenty years ago. For the modern Millennial, you need at least $3,000 set aside for an emergency fund.

The necessity of establishing an emergency fund in your money makeover is a critical part of distancing yourself from the breakeven lifestyle. Most people ignore this advice and continuously dip into their savings account, inhibiting their financial progression. A lack of an emergency cushion removes a protective layer, which could stifle your money makeover.

Your future can change in an instant. A perfect budget can be smashed to pieces by a million variables. Preparing for that eventuality today will soften the blow tomorrow. By establishing a safety net, you will build up your confidence and alleviate the stress of the marginal escape. Save $3,000 for your emergency fund and start protecting yourself now.

Step 2. Build Up a Slush Fund

Once you have $3,000 in your emergency fund, you will be well on your way to gaining financial peace of mind. The next step is to build on your momentum and increase your financial health. In finance, there are a million ratios for determining financial health. The lion's shares of ratios are irrelevant, but one stands out as my favorite: the monthly living expenses covered ratio (covered ratio), or the amount of savings you have accumulated divided by your monthly living expenses.

The covered ratio is a beautiful barometer of financial health. This ratio shows how long you could last without any income. Take a look at your budget from Chapter 3. Your *monthly living expenses* includes expenses such as rent, food, transportation, and utilities. The rule is: The higher your covered ratio, the greater your financial health. Calculate your covered ratio. How long could you last? One month? Two months? A year?

A good rule of thumb is to have a covered ratio between 3 and 6, which would allow you to live off of your savings for three to six months. This is important because it typically takes ninety days to find new employment, thereby providing a fantastic hedge against any unforeseen, or voluntary, unemployment. It is important to point out that your covered ratio does not include your emergency fund. When calculating your covered ratio, only use the amount *above* your emergency fund balance.

The following chart contains a list of financial health categories based on your covered ratio.

Covered Ratio	Financial Health Status
Less than one month	Breakeven
1–3 months	Padding
3–6 months	Slush fund
6–12 months	Options
1–5 years	Bright future
More than 5 years	FU money

Don't get overwhelmed if you are not where you want to be right now. This is simply a snapshot in time. Now that you know your covered ratio, and what it will take to build up your slush fund, you can pursue it aggressively and increase your financial health.

The covered ratio democratizes the appraisal of financial health. If you decrease monthly living expenses and increase savings, you can rapidly improve your financial health. Once you start to climb the ladder of economic health and reach slush-fund status, then it is time to press the accelerator.

Step 3. Reach FU Status

For those readers who want real freedom, you should aim to accelerate your savings and reduce your consumption to accumulate more than six months of living expenses. Once you accomplish this, you can focus on amassing more than a year's worth of living expenses. That is when financial freedom begins to set in and you start absorbing the positive psychological benefits of having money.

The rich life shows itself to those who are persistent and form good financial habits. The magic of the rich life is that it opens up the doors to so much more in life. Instead of focusing on barely getting by, you can focus on becoming a more refined version of yourself.

Reaching FU money status allows you to pursue opportunities as they come across your desk without the cloud of financial considerations. You will have already done your work up front, and now you can reap the rewards of flexibility. Maybe you can finally pursue your passion project full time, tell your bosses to shove it, or take time off to build a new business. In the end, a more substantial covered ratio facilitates more options, peace of mind, and newfound freedom.

Invest Your Ass Off

I can't write a personal finance book without talking about investing. In this section, I am going to cover the basics. As you start to generate momentum with your emergency fund and slush fund, you encroach on a point of critical mass. Once you have your slush fund built with cash, anything after that point should be put to work.

That takes place in the world of investing. The idea of investing is simple: You allow other people to use your money, and you defer consumption. In turn, you accept a rate of return, which varies among different types of investments, and you watch your money grow. It is worth noting that all investing involves some level of risk, so performing your due diligence, weighing your risk tolerance, and understanding your desired rate of return are all vital aspects to successful investing. Although investing involves risk, it is the single greatest way to accumulate wealth over the long run. Investing is how most millionaires become millionaires. It is how the rich remain rich.

To get you started, let's look at some common terms you need to know:

- **Time value of money:** This fundamental investing principle states that money available today (present value), is worth more than the same amount of money in the future (future value) because of its potential earnings capacity.

- **Interest:** This is the charge that a borrower pays to a lender for the privilege of borrowing money. Interest is meant to compensate the lender for their delayed consumption. Usually expressed as a percentage, interest can vary depending upon expected inflation, length of loan, riskiness of borrower, and more.

- **Compound interest:** This is interest paid on the initial principal of a loan plus accumulated interest on the loan. The rate at which compound interest accrues depends upon the number of compounding periods in the loan. For example, a 5 percent semi-annual loan accrues faster than a 10 percent annual loan due to the additional compounding period in the loan.

- **Equity:** Companies are allowed to issue equity, or ownership, in a company to raise capital. Companies do this for all types of reasons—to purchase equipment, invest in research and development, or expand operations. When companies do this, they issue shares of stock for investors to buy.

- **Stock:** The shares of stock a company issues are typically called "common stock" (there are many forms of stock, but for purposes of this book, let's focus on common stock). These fractional pieces of ownership in the company allow investors to receive dividends, participate in company elections, and have an overall say in company operations. Individual investors (you), can buy stocks on exchanges, such as the NYSE, NASDAQ, and LSE. Once you purchase shares of a company, you become what is called a "shareholder."

- **Debt:** If you completed Chapter 2, then you are all too familiar with debt on a personal level. When companies are looking to raise capital (for the same reasons they were in the equity section), they can issue equity or raise debt. Corporate debt is much like personal debt in the way it works, except that when a company is seeking to raise a lot of money in the form of IOUs, they issue what are called "bonds."

- **Bonds:** A bond is a debt security that corporations sell to investors. They are essentially small IOUs, which the company promises to pay back to investors in addition to an interest rate, or reward for lending the money.

- **Certificate of deposit:** A certificate of deposit, or a CD, is a promissory note, typically issued by a bank. These promissory notes are time deposits that limit investor's access to cash for a specified period, or the CD's maturity. CDs range in maturity from only a couple of months to several years. The idea is that you give the bank access to your funds for a certain period of time, during which you cannot use the money. After the CD's maturity has passed, the bank pays you back your principal plus interest.

- **Mutual funds:** A mutual fund is a pool of money aggregated by investors who hire a fund manager to take their cash and make investments on behalf of the fund. There are many different types of funds with different investment objectives: equity funds, bond funds, or money market funds. Investors can buy into a mutual fund at the end of each trading day.

- **Exchange traded funds:** Exchange traded funds, or ETFs, are pools of money that track a group of assets, bonds, or equities. They are like common stock on a stock exchange and can be bought and sold throughout the investing day. They are popular for their low fees and broad diversification.

- **Target date fund:** A target date fund, or a TDF, is a collective investment approach (like ETFs and mutual funds) where the investments chosen by the fund are designed to become more conservative as the "target date" approaches. They are often used to track retirement dates. For example, a TDF 2055 would be a fund allocation mix for a Millennial set to retire by the year 2055.

When it comes to investing the amount of information can be overwhelming, even to seasoned investors. Don't get caught in the vortex of the paradox of choice (Chapter 1). The good news is: Because you are investing, you are winning. Investing allows you to grow your hard-earned capital by leveraging the time value of money and enjoy the bounties of compounding interest. This can grow your wealth at an exponential rate and puts you on the fast track to the rich life.

MILLENNIAL MONEY MAKEOVER PRINCIPLE OF SUCCESS: INVESTING MEANS YOU ARE WINNING

Investing means you are giving yourself a chance at the rich life. By putting your money to work, you begin the process of having your money work for you, instead of you working for your money.

As a young investor, time is on your side. During your twenties and thirties, you have the added benefit of starting your retirement savings early enough to learn from mistakes and make investing a lifelong habit, which is the greatest predictor of becoming rich. Let's learn how to take your investment knowledge and put it to use for the future you (virtually aged to seventy years old).

Money Makeover Pro Tip:
Start Investing Today

Investing means that you are giving your money the opportunity to grow. The following numbers are typical average annual rates of returns for US-based stocks and bonds:[6] S&P 500 Index: 8%; US Corporate Bonds: 5%; Treasury Bill (10 year): 3%

Beginning the Retirement Journey

Most Millennials are indifferent to the idea of retirement. Our limited commitments compound our laissez-faire outlook on life. But when life starts to heat up, and responsibilities begin to accumulate, the idea of retirement suddenly starts to creep back into our peripheral vision.

In the money makeover, we look forward to retirement. Instead of staring up at the peak of retirement in awe, we move out of base camp to begin the journey as soon as possible. We embrace the hike. But Millennials have some catching up to do.

> "The man who moves a mountain begins by
> carrying away small stones."
> —Confucius

A survey conducted by GoBankingRates concluded that 72 percent of Millennials have less than $10,000 in retirement savings.[7] There are a variety of factors that steer people away from retirement saving, but the number-one killer of savings is fear. People often use statements such as, "I don't know how to invest" or "The stock market seems too risky." Fear feeds on itself, so the best way to combat fear is to cut it off early at the pass. Start investing now, and your level of comfort with the concept will skyrocket.

A fundamental principle of investing is: It is not how *much* you start investing but that you *start* investing. In the world of compounding interest, saving as much as $100 or $200 a month can grow into substantial investing over time.

Starting a retirement account is the first step. If you accomplish this step during your twenties or thirties, then you are on the road to success. After that, you can focus on increasing your contributions. According to Cameron Huddleston, a Life+Money columnist for GoBankingRates, "The earlier you start saving, the easier it is—really. Thanks to the power of compounding, if you start regularly setting aside even small amounts as soon as you start working, you could easily have enough for a comfortable retirement."[8]

By investing early, you will not fall behind like the majority of people. Can you imagine the daily anxiety if you were in your fifties and behind on your retirement savings? Well, the problem is more systemic than people realize. Roughly 78 percent of Americans over fifty years old are behind on their retirement savings. Don't get behind on one of the most important long-term decisions of your life.

Retirement Tracker by Age				
Age	Median Income	Retirement Savings Benchmark	Percentage on Track	Percentage Behind
24	$34,605	Started a fund	48%	52%
30	$54,243	$16,273	33%	67%
40	$66,693	$100,040	20%	80%
50	$70,832	$212,496	22%	78%
60	$60,580	$260,494	26%	74%
Source: www.GoBankingRates.com				

Planning for retirement when you are a young professional is the best time to make the conscious decision to save as much as you can. This will alleviate the stress of feeling behind, and it will pave the way for exploration throughout the remainder of your life. Instead of scrambling to stash enough money for retirement in your forties and fifties, you can go on vacations, make memories, and enjoy your peak earning years.

Your relationship with money is incredibly personal. This relationship can define you in more ways than you can imagine. Money orates the tale of who you are, where you come from, and why you are here.

Make your life a great story.

The New Retirement

Googling the phrase "retirement" might make you depressed. According to the first several definitions, which is where most Millennials stop, retirement is "the action or fact of leaving one's job and ceasing to work." How old-fashioned.

Although our economy changed dramatically during the technological revolution of the 2000s, the traditional view of retirement wasn't rebooted. However, Millennials are starting to change that. Most Millennials expect to retire by sixty-two years old, and 40 percent want to semi retire by fifty-seven years old.[9]

Retirement needs a makeover. Instead of sitting around doing nothing during retirement years, Millennials want to pursue passion projects, explore hobbies, engage in activist opportunities, and monetize their skills. They want to fund their desired lifestyles rather than view retirement as a singular stopping point. With this new view, retirement in general needs to be rebranded; it needs *life* injected into it. This new definition of retirement is already marinating in the minds of Millennials, so you might want to define what your future looks like too. This begins with forecasting the future.

What do you want retirement to look like? For some, it may mean part-time consulting, writing, advising, or simply spending time with family. Either way, you should develop clearly stated goals. Saving to save is not an optimal strategy (and really boring). You need intention behind your savings to reinforce the retirement habit loop.

There is no better way to formalize a goal than writing it down. Think about your top five goals and write them out. The following spreadsheet is a great example of goals for your retirement. What are yours? Go to MillennialMoneyMakeover.com for a blank spreadsheet of your own.

Retirement Goals	
Goal 1	Work only three days a week starting at fifty years old.
Goal 2	Travel abroad to different countries at least once a year.
Goal 3	Create a mentor program to stay connected and help my profession.
Goal 4	Own a country home for peace and quiet and a condominium in the city for fun.
Goal 5	Be able to live off of my passive income streams.

Take a look at what you wrote down. Be honest with yourself. Are those *your* goals for retirement, or are those goals embodying what *other* people say should define retirement? If they are not your actual goals, take another shot at writing them down.

The next step is to reverse engineer your path to success. For example, if you wrote down that you wanted to take a European vacation each year, then the travel costs of that annual trip need to be baked into your retirement budget.

During this process, it can be easy to feel overwhelmed. Ignore that sensation.

The fact that you are taking the time *now* to think about where you want to be in thirty to forty years sets you apart from other Millennials. Retirement as a concept needs a makeover. Setting up your goals now gives it the facelift it so desperately needs. Your commitment, your drive, and your dedication to reaching your vision of retirement will help reinvent what retirement means.

Money Makeover Pro Tip:
Investing Consistently Is Enough to Win Big

If you invested $18,500 today into the S&P 500 and contribute that amount every year for thirty-five years, based upon an annualized rate of return of 8 percent, your investments would be worth $3,461,390. Do you think that would fund your desired lifestyle?

Building Your Retirement Accounts

Now that you know the basics of investing, defined retirement goals, and understand the importance of investing early, you need to know what types of accounts to invest in for retirement planning. There are different types of retirement accounts, but like you have been doing throughout the money makeover, you will concentrate on a few to produce maximum results. The following choices describe several different types of retirement accounts, each with pros and cons, which can set you up for long-term wealth and the retirement you deserve.

Roth Individual Retirement Account

For younger investors, beginning a conversation about retirement savings with the Roth individual retirement account

(IRA) only seems fitting. If you are looking for a trusted and advantageous retirement account to get your feet wet in retirement investing, then this is the account for you. The Roth IRA receives a tremendous amount of praise for being the go-to account for younger investors because it offers wonderful long-term advantages.

For the tax year 2018, the IRS allows individuals to contribute up to $5,500 of post tax money into a Roth IRA. As you save for retirement, these contributions have the opportunity to grow tax-free. Better yet, you can invest your contributions in a wide variety of investment vehicles, such as stocks, bonds, ETFs, mutual funds, and more. This flexibility gives new investors the control to invest their money in a wide range of opportunities. Most young investors enjoy this freedom because they are just beginning to determine their risk tolerance.

Another advantage of the Roth IRA is that you are able to pull money out of your account (given certain criteria) without paying a penalty on the withdrawal. But I recommend never doing this. Your retirement accounts should not be used as a crutch for poor financial planning. That is why it is essential to establish an emergency fund and slush fund first—to protect yourself from the temptation to dip into your retirement accounts.

With all of its advantages, the Roth IRA does have some downsides. Once your income exceeds certain IRS limits, you are no longer allowed to contribute to this account. Another disadvantage is that your contributions are limited to $5,500 regardless of how much you want to defer to this account, which caps your capacity for growth. Finally, there is no immediate tax benefit for your contributions.

For retirement planning, you should continue to contribute to your Roth IRA as long as you are not phased out by the IRS income limits. Once you are no longer eligible to contribute to your Roth IRA, then you can move on to the second rung of individual retirement accounts, the Traditional IRA.

Traditional Individual Retirement Account

A conversation about retirement that disregards the Traditional IRA is not a conversation worth continuing. The Traditional IRA is one of the hardest working retirement accounts around. Among retirement aficionados, it is known for its long-term loyalty and continual devotion.

An amazing benefit of the Traditional IRA is the fact that your contributions to this account are never limited by your income or employment. An individual can set up this retirement account and start making contributions immediately.

As of 2018, the Traditional IRA has a contribution limit of $5,500 too. These contributions are also highly flexible and can be invested in a wide range of investment options, similar to the Roth IRA, which is a major advantage to many savers.

However, a major difference between the two retirement accounts is that the money contributed into your Traditional IRA is tax deductible. This means that there is an immediate tax advantage to contributing to this account.

The Traditional IRA does come with some strings attached. Not only do you face the annual contribution limit of $5,500, but you also could face an early withdrawal penalty if you take money out before you are fifty-nine-and-a-half years old. Once you reach retirement age and begin taking distributions, these distributions are taxed as ordinary income. Although you can enjoy the bounties of compounding interest, you are required to make minimum distributions beginning at seventy-and-a-half years old. Luckily, that is a long way off.

An important element to highlight is that the annual contribution limit of $5,500 is split between both of your individual retirement accounts, Roth and Traditional. That means if you contribute $5,500 to one, you cannot contribute to the other.

Once you have maxed out either of your individual retirement accounts, then it is time to move on to your workplace retirement accounts.

Traditional 401(k)

The Traditional 401(k) is my favorite retirement account, bar none.

If you are able to contribute to this account, then do so. The workplace retirement account is a terrific way to supplement your individual retirement accounts. Let's walk through some of the major advantages and disadvantages of the Traditional 401(k).

As the name implies, you can only contribute to a Traditional 401(k) plan if your employer offers this tax-advantaged option to retirement savings. As an added workplace benefit, some employers offer an employer-matching program, meaning that the employer will incentivize employees to save for their retirement by giving those savers matching contributions. The details of the program vary from company to company, but the matching program can act as a catalyst to your retirement savings.

If your employer does not offer a 401(k), I suggest consulting with the head of human resources. It is worth having the conversation to see what the company's plans are for the future. And if your employer is not going to offer a 401(k), then you should continue contributing to your individual retirement account until your employer does provide a 401(k).

	Roth IRA	Traditional IRA	Traditional 401(k)
2018 Contribution limit	$5,500 as a combined IRA limit; $6,500 for those age fifty and above		$18,500 for those under age fifty; $24,500 for those age fifty and above
Account pros	• Individual can set up an account • Large investment selection • Qualified distributions in retirement are tax free • Contributions can be withdrawn at any time • No required minimum distributions in retirement	• Individuals can set up an account • Large investment selection • Contributions can lower taxable income in the year they are made	• High annual contribution limit • Contributions lower taxable income in the year they are made • Employer match, if offered • Eligibility is not limited by income

	Roth IRA	Traditional IRA	401(k)
Account cons	• Lower contribution limits than a 401(k) • No immediate tax benefit for contributions • Contribution ability is phased out at higher incomes	• Lower contribution limits than a 401(k) • Deductions can be phased out at higher incomes if spouse's workplace offers retirement plans • Distributions in retirement are taxed as ordinary income. • Early withdrawals are (before age fifty-nine-and-a-half) subject to a 10% penalty (IRS exceptions apply) • Required minimum distributions begin at age seventy-and-a-half	• Employer must have a 401(k) plan • Lack of control over investment plans and costs • Limited investment selections • Distributions in retirement are taxed as ordinary income, unless a Roth 401(k) • Early withdrawals are (before age fifty-nine-and-a-half) subject to a 10% penalty (IRS exceptions apply) • Required minimum distributions begin at age seventy-and-a-half
***MMM* recommendations**	Fund your Roth IRA until income limit	Fund your Traditional IRA after income limit is reached on your Roth IRA	Max out yearly contributions after you hit your Traditional IRA contribution limit

Assuming your company has a 401(k) plan, one of the first items of business is determining how much of your income you want to allocate to your account. For the tax year 2018, the annual contribution limit for employees was $18,500.

The Traditional 401(k) is ideal for long-term savers because the account imposes a 10 percent penalty for withdrawing money from your 401(k) accounts before you are fifty-nine-and-a-half years old. This forces deferred consumption. Additionally, you are not required to take minimum distributions until you reach seventy-and-a-half years old. A disadvantage of this account is that because your employer creates the account, investment options are typically preselected, thereby limiting your options.

Regardless, you should do everything in your power to maximize your contributions and harness the power of compounding interest. You will also feel the benefits of the tax-deductible contributions once tax season rolls around. That means more money in your pocket!

After you have determined how much to save for retirement, automate the process because it will increase your yields. Just by setting up your accounts and maximizing your contributions you have beaten 99 percent of your peers. The rich life is on its way.

The bottom line is: By contributing to your individual and workplace retirement accounts, you are adopting a rich outlook. As a young investor, time is on your side in this process. You have the added advantage of watching your money grow for decades, which only expands good financial habits. Visualize your feet in the sand and the palm trees waving. Smile, because retirement is going to be a breeze.

Employer Match and Free Money

If your employer offers a 401(k) plan, then you are at a good company. If they offer a company match program, you are at a *great* company. Employer matching programs work when employees put aside a certain percentage of their income, say 5 percent, and the employer will make contributions to your 401(k) in the same amount. My favorite way to help people visualize this is by imagining your boss stopping by your desk every month and handing you a pile of cash simply because you put money into your 401(k) account. The match is a reward for saving and it offers a terrific return on investment.

With a little math, you can see that if you put in 5 percent, and your employer matches you dollar for dollar, you effectively save a total of 10 percent!

> *"Diligence is the mother of good fortune."*
> —Miguel de Cervantes, *Don Quixote*

If you have reservations about saving with a 401(k), you should contribute up to your employer's match *at a minimum*. Otherwise, you are leaving free money on the table.

To effectively capture the unbelievable power of compounding interest, saving early, the employer match, and long-term planning, let's examine two saving scenarios.

Scenario 1: Compounding Colin works for Matching Monsters Inc., a factory for children's toys, earning a salary of $75,000. As part of a management training program, he has the option to contribute to a 401(k) plan with a 5 percent dollar-for-dollar match. Compounding Colin decides to contribute the annual IRS contribution limit of $18,500 and also enjoy the benefits of the company's matching program.

Scenario 2: Lazy Larry, Compounding Colin's manager, does quite well for himself and earns a six-figure salary of $150,000. He lives large and is not that concerned about retirement. As a result, he only contributes up to the company's matching percentage.

Let's see how the two savers perform after thirty years on the job in the chart on page 181.

Both savers have captured the power of compounding interest. However, Compounding Colin has dedicated himself to maxing out his 401(k) contributions, whereas Lazy Larry only took advantage of the company match. With time, the chasm between the two savers is gigantic. Although Lazy Larry may have been Compounding Colin's boss, it is safe to say that Compounding Colin saved like a boss.

....

Millennial Money Makeover Principle of Success: Time Is Always On Your Side

As a young investor, you have the added benefit of allowing your money to grow for decades. The longer compound interest has to work, the greater your return on investment. Time is on your side.

....

Savings Gives You Freedom and Purpose

Mastering your finances will lead you to your true calling. Defeating debt has a tremendous effect on the psyche. Saving an emergency fund seems to numb the worries of daily financial issues. Building up a substantial retirement savings makes the future transparent. This mental peace grants you the ability to focus on your purpose in life.

Being financially fit will allow you to excel in your career.

Retirement Savings Accumulation Table

Employment Length	Compounding Colin: Salary $75,000			Lazy Larry: Salary $150,000		
	Annual Contribution	Company Match	Total Retirement	Annual Contribution	Company Match	Total Retirement
Year 1	$18,500	$2,500	$21,000	$5,000	$5,000	$10,000
Year 5	$18,500	$2,500	$118,379	$5,000	$5,000	$56,371
Year 10	$18,500	$2,500	$276,797	$5,000	$5,000	$131,808
Year 15	$18,500	$2,500	$488,795	$5,000	$5,000	$232,760
Year 20	$18,500	$2,500	$772,497	$5,000	$5,000	$367,856
Year 25	$18,500	$2,500	$1,152,155	$5,000	$5,000	$548,645
Year 30	$18,500	$2,500	$1,660,222	$5,000	$5,000	$790,582

*This assumes a 6 percent annual rate throughout the thirty years of contribution and no withdrawals from the account.

This fitness makes the risks of starting your own business or venture seem less daunting. Perhaps you already love what you do, and gunning for that promotion or making that next sales pitch seems a little easier when the risk of financial failure is removed from the picture.

Creating a life in which you don't have to worry about tomorrow allows you to seize new opportunities. This life allows you to accept projects or opportunities you previously could not afford.

Money points to tangible progress. Although you shouldn't be focused on money alone, recognizing that having money creates opportunity is key to financial progression. Allow yourself the security of no debt, cash savings, investments, and retirement savings, and suddenly chasing after your passions seems like a matter of necessity.

Action Items

Hopefully, this chapter has taught you at least two critical pieces of valuable information: Investing means you are winning, and time is on your side. The future is full of retirement millionaires; the question is whether you are going to be one of them. Investing early and often is the surest path to financial freedom.

When you are starting to accumulate your cash and investments, remember to follow these steps to grow your riches quickly.

1. Understand that you are your own worst enemy.

2. Build up your emergency and slush funds.

3. Start investing early and let your seeds grow.

4. Set your retirement goals and create your bridge to reach them.

5. Allocate as much as you can to build the retirement you deserve.

Now that you have a clear vision of how to put your financial house in order, it is time to learn how to use technology to increase your chances of success. In the next chapter, you will learn about the rise of robo-advisors and why you should use them, develop an automated financial ecosystem that will optimize your financial growth, find the right money management approach, and understand the essential elements of the rich life.

When it comes to your money makeover, it is important to highlight that what you are investing in is less important than starting the process altogether. As Burton Malkiel, author of *A Random Walk Down Wall Street,* says, "Put time on your side. Start investing early and save regularly. Live modestly and don't touch the money that's been set aside."[11] Above all, have fun with picking your investments, and focus on long-term capital appreciation.

Technology is about to make this exponentially better.

6

....

The Power of Automation: Leveraging Technology to Reach the Rich Life

*The real problem is not whether machines
think but whether men do.*
—B. F. Skinner

The rich don't think about money.

Well, not all the time. When they do think about money, they contemplate it in a rich way. They think about maximizing their returns, reducing risk, paying low management fees, and building a financial ecosystem that works for them, day and night. The rich think about automating their money.

Successful business leaders and philosophers often opine on the acute benefits of habit and daily routine. Minting momentum in money management is no different. So far, you have learned about the massive benefits of building better financial habits. In this chapter, you are going to explore how to reap the harvest of cumulative advantage, focus on outsourcing your financial decisions, and learn to invest on a consistent basis.

These two modern pearls of the wealthy, routine and automation, have been have proven to be the gifts that keep on giving. Mastering the automation process and outsourcing the chores necessary to build wealth is a rich decision.

Once your financial ecosystem is constructed properly, you will be able to focus on calibrating your wealth-generating machine. Automating your finances is one of the easiest steps you can take to drastically change your financial future. It will provide you with the infrastructure to handle everything that you should already be doing without lifting a finger. The time has come to let the professionals work for you and leverage technology to accelerate your path to the rich life.

Master Your Rice

In the documentary *Jiro Dreams of Sushi,* eighty-five-year-old head chef Jiro Ono details out his daily routine, which he has been following for over forty years. His focus on routine has allowed him to relentlessly concentrate on perfecting his craft, one day at a time.[1] Jiro passes this worldview on to his apprentices, who often have to spend years mastering how to cook the basics of sushi, like rice. This tireless dedication and pursuit of perfection has paid off. Jiro's sushi restaurant has become internationally recognized. Celebrity notables, such as former president Barack Obama, have visited Jiro's eight-seat restaurant in Tokyo for a taste of the world-famous sushi.

Jiro continually stresses the importance of sticking to a daily routine. In fact, he credits his success to that consistency, and if he finds himself falling out of that routine, he takes drastic measures to ensure he falls back into his daily cadence.

Although not all of us will become world-renowned chefs, Jiro's routine provides a relevant analogy: Success is bred in schedule. The consistency of routine allows the mind the necessary time for exploration. Whether you are trying to form a new habit or break an old one, your ability to create a good routine will define your success.

It is much the same with your finances. Most people haphazardly approach their money management. They watch month in and month out as their paychecks hit their bank accounts, only to find at the end of the month they have nothing left. To give success a chance, this undisciplined approach must stop.

You cannot expect to manage the growth of your money well if you have no cadence to your approach. In the past decade, there has been an explosion of growth in innovative companies whose core mission is to help people solve the problem. This movement has given individuals the power to automate their finances and increase their chances of long-term success. Leveraging the power of technology has never been easier. In this chapter, you are going to learn how to practice good financial habits, keep to a routine, and in the end, master your rice.

The Triple D

Automating your financial decisions gives you the advantage of maintaining a consistent approach. By doing this, you protect yourself against decision fatigue. Continuously deciding when to pay off your debt, how much money to invest, the percent to allocate to each fund, or whether to invest at all erodes your willpower.

Human behavior is a funny thing; we can change our habits virtually overnight by creating the appropriate framework for success. The best way to execute creating a money system that works is to implement what I call the Triple D: design, delegate, and defer.

Design

The first step to set up your money flow system is to design its overall structure. You need to have a handle on your accounts—savings, credit cards, student loans, and retirement. This provides the scaffolding to construct the perfect system.

Once you have a clear understanding of where you want your money to go each month, you can begin designing your system to reach your short-term and long-term goals. For example, if you are going to save 10 percent of your take-home pay, then construct an automatic deposit of 10 percent from your paycheck into a savings or investment account.

Delegate

Once you have designed your money flow system, you need to become comfortable with delegating responsibility. There is no need to check your savings or investment account each day, each month, or even each year. Instead, have faith in the system that you constructed in the design step and delegate the responsibility of moving money around to your system. Outsource that headache. This will free your mind of worry and reduce the manual errors caused by human interaction. Let the machines do the heavy lifting.

Defer

Now that you have designed a beautiful money flow system and delegated virtually all thoughts of monthly management, the final step is to defer as much of your income as possible to the future. The wonder of money flow systems is that they trick you psychologically. Embrace this hack.

For example, if you make $5,000 per month and designate $1,500 to your 401(k), $1,000 toward automated rent payments, $300 to your slush fund, $100 to your emergency fund, and $100 to your vacation fund, you are left with $2,000 of guilt-free spending money for the month. Enjoy this money and spend it passionately.

....

MILLENNIAL MONEY MAKEOVER PRINCIPLE OF SUCCESS: TECHNOLOGY IS MEANT TO BE LEVERAGED

Use the fulcrum of technology to accelerate your wealth generation. This means using websites, software, and automated systems to increase your chance of achieving and exceeding your financial goals.

....

Create a Flowchart to Help You Dominate

As a budding CPA, there is no way to get around taking some rather dry accounting classes. The more mundane courses revolved around internal controls and flowcharts. During these lectures, it was all I could do to keep my eyes open. They consisted of monotone professors mapping out detailed business processes and converting those processes into visual schematics. These classes were artwork for accountants. As you can imagine, this was nothing short of terrible. Flowcharts were my least favorite topic.

But that all changed one day when I made the connection between automating my finances and the value of flowcharts. From that point, I understood the beauty of a well-crafted and efficient flowchart.

You too can appreciate this beauty by mapping out your monthly money flow chart. The process begins with a holistic view of all of your sources of income, checking accounts, savings accounts, retirement accounts, and savings goals. Luckily, all you have to do is flip back to Chapter 3 and take a look at your passion budget. This will provide you with everything you need to get started.

Depending on where you are in your money makeover, the following list can give you a good idea of the accounts you should have set up.

- Checking account
- Savings account
- Emergency fund
- Slush fund
- Roth IRA
- Traditional IRA
- Traditional 401(k)
- Investment account

Open these in succession of your money makeover progress. Once you have your accounts set up, you can get started designing your money flow system. This is the fun part.

List Your Accounts

One of the first questions you should ask yourself when getting your finances in order is: Where is all of my money? You should be able to recite an itemized list of your accounts and fund balances. This should include all of your checking accounts, savings accounts, emergency fund, Roth IRA, Traditional IRA, and Traditional 401(k). After all of your money is accounted for, the next task is to gather all of the information in one area. Keeping it consolidated makes for easy maintenance.

Download the following spreadsheet at MillennialMoney Makeover.com to help with organization during this process.

Flowchart Account Login Information			
Account Type	Institution	Website	Password
Checking account			
Savings account			
Emergency fund			
Slush fund			
Roth IRA			
Traditional IRA			
Traditional 401(k)			
Investment accounts			

It is surprising how consolidating all of your financial information improves your spirit. You will find that reducing clutter and streamlining accounts is great for your long-term well-being. This newly constructed repository acts as the heart of your centralized operating system.

Now that all of your login information is in one location, you can concentrate on trying to reduce the number of institutions holding your money. Personally, I have my Roth IRA, Traditional IRA, employee stock, and investment accounts all at one brokerage. This helps me coordinate all of my retirement and investment accounts in one place and reduces the headache of managing multiple logins. Another advantage is that it allows me to see all of my money in one spot, which always makes me smile.

Connect the Dots

Having all of your accounts aggregate in one location is help-ful, but only if you use this efficiency to your advantage. To do this, you need to link your checking account to the rest of your financial structure in the correct order. This is where overall design meets delegation.

Linking your accounts to your financial infrastructure should be done in the proper order, mirroring your make-over progression. Most payment processing systems give you the ability to link your paycheck to multiple accounts. Let's review how to set up each of the five funds flow.

Link Your Checking to Your Credit Card and Student Loans

If you have debt, the first step is to link your credit cards to your checking account. You can do this by logging into your credit card's website and scheduling an automatic monthly payment. If you are trying to pay off credit card debt aggres-sively, make the automatic payments in your "stretch zone." To ensure you don't incur overdraft fees, scheduled your payments for one or two days *after* your paycheck hits your checking account.

If you have student loans to pay off, the concept is the same. Schedule automatic payments from your checking ac-count. Put as much as you can toward these balances. You will thank yourself later for being aggressive today.

Link Your Checking to Your Emergency Fund

Accidents, injuries, and layoffs are an inevitable part of life. Money makeover graduates hedge against this reality. An excellent way to avoid financial submersion after an emergency is to plan for the crisis *now*. That is where your $3,000 emergency fund from Chapter 5 comes into play.

After you are debt free, you will start contributing regularly to your emergency fund, which you can set up at your bank. This account should be connected to your checking account and will be the holding spot for your emergency fund. Your goal should be to pad this account regularly to prepare for the unexpected. Once you surpass the recommended $3,000 in your emergency fund, you can continue to make small contributions.

Link Your Checking to Your Slush Fund Account

When your money flow system is ready, you can link your checking account to a new savings account. This account is in addition to your emergency fund account and should be at a separate institution than your checking and emergency fund. This will ensure you don't raid this account in a moment of weakness.

Once you set up this new account, make sure that your slush fund and checking account are linked to one other, can perform transfers for no fee, and have a low minimum balance threshold. To make sure your idle cash is garnering some momentum find savings accounts with high annual percentage yields (APYs).

The power of linking these accounts comes when you want to schedule automatic transfers and manage your cash flow. Your goal with this account is to reach a monthly expense covered ratio between 3 and 6 (refer to Chapter 5). Once you meet this goal, it will be time to start investing the extra cash.

Link Your Checking to Your Retirement Funds

Once you have set up your Roth IRA, Traditional IRA, Traditional 401(k), and investment accounts, the next step is to start making healthy contributions. Don't fall into the trap of thinking that you don't need to set up these accounts because you can't start saving for retirement. Even if you are only putting away $100 a month, it is still better than nothing.

Construct an automatic deposit from your paycheck to these accounts. Most payroll providers have this capability and can make real-time deductions. Remember to make them *before* money gets routed to your checking account. This is essential when saving for retirement. If you don't see the money hit your checking account, you won't be tempted to spend it.

Link Your Checking to Your Happy Money

This is by far everyone's favorite account. Your happy money account is your savings account for that upcoming trip, vacation, or wedding that you are preparing for. This account is for what you daydream about at work.

To achieve this, set up a checking account and name it something fun. Then, allocate money to the account based off of your goals. This happy money account comes last because you should always focus on making sure your foundation is cemented—no debt, cash for emergencies, and retirement savings—before going on vacation. That way you can enjoy it stress free.

Percentage Allocation

Once you know what your fully constructed money flow system will look like, you can focus on determining the percentage of income you want transported to each account.

Refer back to Chapter 3 during which you built your passion budget. What percentage of your income did you set aside for paying off credit cards, student loans, savings, or happy spending? Let's discuss three common scenarios with benchmarked goals for allocating your expenses. Download a blank version at MillennialMoneyMakeover.com to record your own plan.

Percent Allocation Scenarios			
Expense type	Credit card repayment plan	Student loan repayment plan	Accumulation plan
Rent	20%	20%	20%
Variable expenses	30%	30%	25%
Credit card payments	.30%	15%	0%
Student loan payments	15%	30%	0%
Retirement	0%	0%	35%
Cash savings	5%	5%	20%
Total	100%	100%	100%

The milestone you are on in your money makeover will determine which plan is right for you. For example, if you have $7,000 in credit card debt to repay, then begin with the credit card repayment plan. Are you saddled with annoying student loans? Then concentrate your efforts on the student loan repayment plan. Once you are debt free, turn your attention to the accumulation plan. This will help you build as much wealth as possible. Be aggressive and be bold enough in the beginning so that you can pull yourself back later.

Once you set up all of your accounts and start to link your income accounts to your savings account, the proportion of benefit to effort will lean in your favor. In other words, if you concentrate on setting up your accounts right the first time, you will reap the tremendous reward of automation. The following diagram takes a look at an example of a fully constructed money flow system.

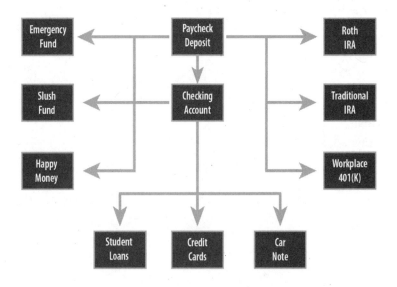

Now that you have your financial ecosystem running in synchronization, it is time to focus on growing the nest egg that you started in Chapter 5. Once you have accumulated enough hard-earned cash to fully fund an emergency fund and slush fund, it is time to put any extra savings to work. The world of investing can be confusing, but there are professionals here to help.

The Rise of Robo-Advisors

In our modern economy, the use of technology is ubiquitous. From leveraging the latest software to making businesses run more efficiently to harnessing the power of robotics in the surgery room, the benefits gained from the historic advancement in technology over the past several decades have been tremendous. The next frontier for machine learning and algorithms lies in the FinTech, or financial technology, community and has the capacity to disrupt the entire financial advice and wealth management industries.

Human financial advisors have long been the conduit for receiving sophisticated, albeit expensive, financial advice. In recent years, human financial advisors have leveraged robo-advisors to deliver on client expectations but only behind the scenes. Robo-advisors—a class of financial advisors that provides automated financial services online by using software programs and algorithms to provide financial advice and investment management services—were commonly used among human financial advisors who were juggling large books of business and using robo-advisors to reduce their workload.[2]

In the wake of the great recession, robo-advisors finally wheeled out from behind the desk and plugged into the mainstream financial services community. In 2008, robo-advisors were delivered straight to consumers with a lack of human intermediates, and the response has been unprecedented. But this acceptance was a long time coming.

During the early 2000s, there was shift in online consumer behavior. Consumers were becoming remarkably familiar with the Internet, and its proliferation into our economy largely changed the way we conduct business, interact socially, learn new information, and manage money. Digitally native Millennials helped spur the trend in how consumers share personal information online and the reduced the previous anxiety around divulging private information to online businesses. As a result, Millennials have a propensity to share personal information—age, location, profession, salary, and financial goals—if they believe they will receive a superior product or service in return. In fact, 57 percent of Millennials are prepared to share their detailed savings plans and targets with others if they perceive that doing so would offer a more tailored approach to reaching their financial goals.[3] Queue the propagation of support for robo-advisors in the investment community.

Silicon Valley woke up to this changing trend in 2006 with the success of Mint, an online semi-automated personal finance management business. In 2009, Aaron Patzer, the founder of Mint, sold his company to Intuit for $170 million and provided the necessary proof of concept to investors and entrepreneurs.[4] Robo-advising and the digital age of investing were here to stay.

After robo-advising crossed into the collective mainstream consumer consciousness as a viable alternative to human financial advisors, a significant industry shift began to take place. New companies like Betterment, which made a splashing debut at TechCrunch Disrupt in 2008, began to pave the way for the robo-advising industry as they saw a massive opportunity in the marketplace to make investing simple. Jon Stein, the founder of Betterment, says he started his company to "tell you how much to invest and manage your money for you, all throughout your life, in a way that gives you better outcomes. We do it all so that you don't have to."[5] As the market opportunity became clear, more established financial services players, like Vanguard and Charles Schwab, began to pivot to offer this newly desired service. Since then, the flood of assets under management into robo-advising companies has been unprecedented.

In the early days, robo-advisors helped retail investors with automated asset allocation and portfolio management. And as technology improved, so too has the flood of competition to democratize financial services previously only offered to the rich. Elite services such as tax-loss harvesting, detailed planning for college savings, and cash-flow management are now available at scale to consumers for a fraction of their former cost.

The case for using robo-advisors is garnering massive support as the benefits that such technologies provide to young investors, and those looking to get their financial house in order, continue to surge. Additionally, advocates point out that this technology offers superior advantages from the traditional "Do It Yourself" investment approach.[6] Millennials are taking note by augmenting robo-advice with conventional human interaction, which seems to be a successful strategy for improving their financial position.

As the advancement in wealth management software continues, the incremental progress will lead to an automating of the financial services industry. There are now tremendous benefits to using robo-advisors, several of which we will examine in the next section. As these financial services scale, costs will continue to decrease, and you will have information previously reserved for the rich right at your fingertips.

....

Money Makeover Pro Tip:
Use Financial Technology to Improve Your Life

Check out companies offering robo-advising, wealth advisory services, and online financial tools such as:

- Betterment

- Wealthfront

- Personal Capital

These companies are dedicated to the idea of making investing simple and alleviating the traditional cost of the old financial advisor business model. Let them help you get to the rich life.

....

Four Reasons You Should Use Robo-Advising

Robo-advising is the wave of the future in money management. The financial management industry is scrambling to keep up with the flood of money pouring into this segment of the market, as investors are placing their money on technological improvements in a historically opaque money management industry. The old gatekeepers are soon to be ousted by a more refined, technologically advanced, and appealing way of managing money.

A recent study by consulting firm Deloitte estimated that "assets under automated management" in the United States will grow from the present $300 billion to a staggering $5–$7 trillion by 2025.[7] This growth would represent between 10 and 15 percent of the total retail financial assets under management. Here are four reasons many investors, Millennials among them, are clamoring toward this new wave of money management—and why you might be drawn to it too.

1. Ease of Use

Technology is ubiquitous in young investors' daily lives. Millennials are plugged into the digital world. It is no surprise that the traditional means of finding a financial advisor seems outdated to this cohort.

Recognizing this market opportunity, investment companies have started to offer robo-advising, which is an automated way investment platforms use algorithms to allocate, invest, and manage investors' funds. Robo-advising takes the inefficiencies of human interaction out of the equation and leverages investors' risk appetite with technology to offer a robust investing strategy.

Companies that use robo-advising have made the process extremely user friendly, increasing its overall appeal. To get started, potential investors can simply visit a website and fill out an automated sign-up form. Once investors complete the onboarding phase, they can begin investing and regularly check in on their investment performance. Additionally, many robo-advisors offer investors a transparent and easily accessible investment management portal, which includes analytics, fund performance, transparent fee schedules, and portfolio allocation.

2. Lower Management Fees

Robo-advisors are offering this innovative service for a fraction of the traditional investment management cost.

Historically, investment management fees are made off a portion of assets under management, or AUM. These fees usually ranged from 1 to 2 percent of AUM and were meant to compensate the investment manager for their analysis, insights, trades, and overall market advice. Robo-advisors have slashed these fees.

Fees for robo-advising range well below 1 percent of AUM, typically hovering around 0.50 percent, or four times lower than the traditional means of investment management.[8] Lower investment fees matter because they can have a material impact on your investment performance over the long haul.

3. Automated Investment Process

Another major attraction of robo-advisors is that the investment process is automated. This allows investors to access benefits that were previously only utilized by the wealthy. Two main strategies automated in robo-advising are automatic rebalancing and tax-loss harvesting.[9]

Automatic rebalancing is the process of dynamically realigning the weight of a portfolio of investments. As an investor, you choose your desired level of risk allocation, which is then baked into your portfolio by spreading your investments among different risk categories to meet your original risk appetite. When the market fluctuates, your level of investment performance changes with it. The rebalancing process ensures that your portfolio retains your original risk allocation, which could mean selling overexposed areas like stock and acquiring less risky investments like bonds.

Tax-loss harvesting is another significant advantage to robo-advising. This process occurs when an investment is sold at a loss. Those losses are "harvested," or kept to offset future taxable gains. This process optimizes your portfolio's return. Tax-loss harvesting, along with tax advantaged investment strategies, have the ability to add as much as 1 percent a year in value to your portfolio. Accumulated over your investment life, this can boost your overall returns, letting you keep more of your money.

The automated process of investing and the advantages of digital advising have led many investors to question the value of traditional financial advisors. With this decline in value perception, there appears to be a shift to commoditize financial planning.[10] This means Millennials will quickly gain access to sophisticated investing technology, which will help them invest more, early, and often.

4. Lower Balances and Maintenance

Robo-advising is perfect for a certain type of investor: one who has a demanding career or family life and doesn't have the time to focus on money management. Additionally, it allows investors to outsource the bulk of the money management process for a fraction of the traditional cost.

For young investors, robo-advisors offer another carrot: low minimum account balances. A traditional investment advisor can require a high minimum balance to get started, some as high as $200,000, leaving many potential clients behind. That is where robo-advising has gained ground. Some robo-advisors require no minimums, while others offer professional investment management on balances of $5,000 or more.[11]

Investing means you are winning. Being able to allocate your money to a robo-advisor can free an investor's time to do other things. This outsourcing allows investors to maintain piece of mind and put other people to work, no matter how much you have to invest.

Millennials' attitude toward technology and investing seems to create a perfect scenario for robo-advising. However, robo-advising is not right for everyone. Do your research and investigate which robo-advising companies are right for you, if any.

For those looking to invest hard-earned cash after they have built their emergency fund and slush fund, robo-advisors or a more traditional route can accelerate your wealth creation. By learning how to get both investment professionals and technology on your side, you are beginning to act like the wealthy.

Money Makeover Pro Tip:
Let Professionals Build Your Wealth

Investment professionals specialize in growing your wealth. Whether it is determining your optimal risk tolerance, selecting investments, or allocating your portfolio, receiving professional advice is a trick of the wealthy now available to you.

Modern Money Management

Whereas the shift in demand to robo-advising is certainly garnering tremendous attention from industry experts, many companies are honing in on the strategy of the future: a hybrid approach of robo-advisors and personal investment management. Investment managers and advisors know that they need more than just algorithms to win over Millennials. This intersection, where algorithmic investing meshes with human intellect, is a terrific place for you to thrive. This is the modern approach to money management.

Personal interaction, or the human side of the business, is still a critical part in the investment process, and it gives the hybrid model a tremendous advantage. The human touch to investing can be powerful for your portfolio because financial advisors and investment experts can offer a catered approach to help you determine your risk appetite, pick specific investments, assist in retirement planning, resolve nuanced tax and estate planning, and allow you to implement a holistic and synchronized approach in order for you to achieve your long-term goals.

MILLENNIAL MONEY MAKEOVER PRINCIPLE OF SUCCESS: THE RICH LIFE IS ABOUT MORE THAN MONEY

Being rich allows your mind to focus on becoming the best version of yourself. It entitles you to pursue your hopes and dreams without the added pressure of financial failure. The rich life opens doors.

Millennials are highly inquisitive when it comes to investing and wealth generation. Knowing that they have someone (literally) on their side allows for a more confident and coordinated investment philosophy. It alleviates the fear of the unknown. Investment professionals are lining up in droves to help Millennials manage their money because Millennials are now entering a period of reaching many of life's milestones. Millennials also stand as benefactors to a historic shift in wealth during the next several decades.

Professionalizing your approach now can be the catalyst you need for maximizing your wealth accumulation. Get the professionals on your side early to help bolster your returns. The investment community is awash with talented individuals waiting to help accelerate your path to the rich life.

Action Items

Hopefully, this chapter taught you the value of automating your finances and outsourcing the decision of money management. By leveraging technology to accelerate your growth, learning how to build the perfect money flow system, and working with investment professionals, you have reached the last milestone of your money makeover.

When implementing these steps, remember the following items:

1. Recognize that mastering your money takes time, practice, and intention.

2. Design your financial ecosystem for success.

3. Implement your automated money flow system.

4. Get professionals and technology on your side.

5. Win the long game.

Your money makeover is now complete. You have received the tools for financial success. But this book ends where it began. Knowing the path to complete the money makeover is only half the battle. The challenge and decision is yours alone. It is up to you to act, change your financial life, and keep momentum on your side. Continue your progress and secure the rich life. Do not wait. Do it now.

Welcome to your financial awakening.

Conclusion:
Winning the Long Game

If this book has taught you anything, it is that you have the power to master your money. Whether you are currently buried in student loans, just starting to build a budget, or already accumulating your emergency fund and investments, everyone starts from the same place.

The decision to turn professional and learn about the intersection of life and money is a transformational one. When you began the money makeover, you might have thought that your transformation had an end point. The reality is that mastering money is a continuous journey, full of highs and lows, which will help you improve every day. Embracing this journey allows you to live your best life.

The rich life is sought by many but attained by few. You are different. You will be among the few that take the necessary steps to gain the financial freedom that you deserve. This will change your life forever and put you on a new path.

This path ushers in a new kind of responsibility. It calls on you to help others along the way and enjoy the rewards of the rich life. The truly rich give more than they take, not worrying about what they receive in return. They know that money is not the end goal. They are driven by something more profound: devotion to their passions and calling.

Wherever you are in your money makeover, keep the Millennial Money Makeover principles close by and remember to follow the sequence necessary to achieve financial freedom. Decide to turn professional and make it permanent. Pay off all of your debts as quickly as possible, and resist the temptation to get tangled again. Create and refine your budget. Optimize the large-ticket purchases you will make early in life to set yourself up for long-term success. Build a financial cushion to distance yourself from the breakeven lifestyle and live a fully present and forward-thinking life. Invest when everyone else is spending and grow your wealth. The momentum of your money makeover will take over. The rich life is waiting.

MILLENNIAL MONEY MAKEOVER
BONUS MATERIAL

When I started the concept for this book, I had no idea where it would go. My goal was to write a book that would give my readers a step-by-step guide for financial success. Since then, the response has been tremendous.

If you are like most of my readers, you want more. As with any makeover, once the transformation is complete, you are left yearning for the next major money milestone. If you have any questions about Millennial Money Makeover, feel free to contact me on my blog, MillennialMoneyMakeover.com, send me an email at Conor@millennialmoneymakeover.com, or find me on one of my socials (Twitter: Conor_Rich; Facebook: TheConorRichardson).

If you have read this far and want to know more, get access to special bonus material, such as interviews with investment professionals, in-depth analysis on key makeover principles, and real world success stories, by sending an email directly to bonusmaterial@millennialmoneymakeover.com.

As always, thanks for reading.

Notes

Introduction

1. Annamaria Lusardi and Carlo de Bassa Scheresberg. "Gen Y Personal Finances: A Crisis of Confidence and Capability," May 6, 2014. *http://gflec.org/wp-content/uploads/2015/01/a738b9_b453bb8368e248f1b-c546bb257ad0d2e.pdf*

2. Ibid.

3. *http://quoteinvestigator.com/2016/07/20/knowledge/*

4. Thomas Stanley and William Danko. *The Millionaire Next Door: The Surprising Secrets of America's Wealthy.* Maryland: Taylor Trade Publishing, 2010.

5. Kim Shandrow. "Billionaire Chris Sacca on the 'Quickest Way to Get Rich," *Entrepreneur,* June 27, 2016. *www.entrepreneur.com/article/278130*

Chapter 1

1. Tanya Korobka. "Why 70 Percent of Millennials Are Unhappy With Their Jobs," *SheKnows*, November 02, 2015. *www.sheknows.com/living/articles/1100749/why -70-percent-of-millennials-are-unhappy-with-their-jobs*

2. Daniel Pink. *Drive: The Surprising Truth About What Motivates Us*. New York: Penguin Publishing Group, 2011.

3. Ryan Holiday and Stephen Hanselman. *The Daily Stoic: 366 Mediations on Wisdom, Perseverance, and the Art of Living*. New York: Penguin Random House, 2016.

4. Mark Cuban. *How to Win at the Sport of Business: If I Can Do It, You Can Do It*. New York: Diversion Books, 2011.

5. Sheena Iyengar and Mark Lepper. "When Choice is Demotivating: Can One Desire Too Much of a Good Thing?" *Journal of Personality and Social Psychology* 79, no. 6 (2000): 995–1006.

6. Seth Godin. *The Dip: A Little Book that Teaches You When to Quit (and When to Stick)*. New York: Penguin Publishing Group, 2007.

7. Josh Waitzkin. *The Art of Learning: An Inner Journey to Optimal Performance*. New York: Free Press, 2008.

8. Tim Ferris. "Shay Carl—From Manual Laborer to 2.3 Billion YouTube Views," June 26, 2016. *http://tim. blog/2016/06/27/shay-carl/*

9. Charles Duhigg. *The Power of Habit: Why We Do What We Do in Life and Business*. New York: Random House Publishing Group, 2014.

10. Jesse Yomtov. "Full List of Every Olympic Medal Michael Phelps Has Won," *USA Today*. August 7, 2016. *www.usatoday.com/story/sports/olympics/rio -2016/2016/08/07/michael-phelps-medals/88361712/*

11. Rachel Dicker. "Watch a 15-year-old Michael Phelps Discuss His Goals for the Future," *U.S. News*. August 15, 2016. *www.usnews.com/news/articles/2016-08-15/ watch-a-15-year-old-michael-phelps-discuss-his -goals-for-the-future*

Chapter 2

1. Steven Pressfield. *The War of Art: Break Through the Blocks and Win Your Inner Creative Battles*. New York: Black Irish Books, 2002.

2. Kelly Dilworth. "Rate Survey: Average Card APR Rises to All-time High of 15.59 Percent," *CreditCards. com*. March 22, 2017. *www.creditcards.com/credit- card-news/interest-rate-report-32217-up-2121.php*

3. Maria Lamagna. "Americans Now Have the Highest Credit Card Debt in U.S. History," *MarketWatch*. August 8, 2017. *www.marketwatch.com/story/us -households-will-soon-have-as-much-debt-as-they -had-in-2008-2017-04-03*

4. Ibid.

5. Kantar Media. 2016. *www.statista.com/statis tics/308842/ad-spend-credit-card-issuers-usa/*

6. Jamie Gonzalez-Garcia. "Credit Card Ownership Sta- tistics," *CreditCards.com*. October 25, 2016. *www.cred itcards.com/credit-card-news/ownership-statistics.php*

7. Jeffrey Scott. "Millennials Still Want Credit Cards," *FICO.com.* June 9, 2016. *www.fico.com/en/newsroom/fico -survey-millennials-still-want-credit-cards-06-09-2016*

8. Kathleen Elkins. "Here Is How Much the Average Millennial Has in Savings," CNBC. September 14, 2017. *www.cnbc.com/2017/09/14/how-much-money -the-average-millennial-has-in-savings.html*

9. Matthew Frankel. "How American Express Company Makes Most of Its Money," *The Motley Fool.* July 25, 2017. *www.fool.com/investing/2017/07/25/how-amer ican-express-company-makes-most-of-its-mon.aspx*

10. Jessica Dickler. "Credit Card Debt Hits a Record High. It's Time to Make a Payoff Plan," CNBC. January 23, 2018. *www.cnbc.com/2018/01/23/credit-card -debt-hits-record-high.html*

11. "Do You Need Multiple Credit Cards?" *Bettermoney habits.com. https://bettermoneyhabits.bankofamerica. com/en/credit/having-multiple-credit-cards*

12. Erin Issa. "2017 American Household Credit Card Debt Study," NerdWallet. December 10, 2017. *www.nerdwa llet.com/blog/average-credit-card-debt-household/*

13. Jay Boyer. "The 'Snowball Approach' to Debt," North-western Kellogg School of Management. August 12, 2012. *www.kellogg.northwestern.edu/news_arti cles/2012/snowball-approach.aspx*

14. "Annual Percentage Rate—APR," *Investopedia.com. www.investopedia.com/terms/a/apr.asp?lgl=myfinance layout-no-ads*

15. "Teary-Eyed Student Loan Officers Proudly Watch As $200,000 Asset Graduates From College," *The*

Onion. May 09, 2016. *https://local.theonion.com/ teary-eyed-student-loan-officers-proudly-watch -as-200-1819578870*

16. Nick Clements. "The Real Student Loan Crisis: Debt-Fueled Tuition Inflation," *Forbes.* August 8, 2016. *www.forbes.com/sites/nickclements/2016/08/08/ the-real-student-loan-crisis-debt-fueled-tuition -inflation/#4b85a90d6824*

17. Selena Maranjian. "7 Common Expenses Growing Much Faster than Inflation," *CNN Money.* August 4, 2017. *http://money.cnn.com/2017/08/02/pf/expenses -inflation/index.html*

18. Ingrid Lunden. "Student Loan Platform CommonBond Raises $300M and $30M in Equity, Buys Gradible," *TechCrunch.* July 19, 2016. *https://tech crunch.com/2016/07/19/student-loan-platform -commonbond-raises-300m-and-30m-in-equity-buys -gradible/*

19. Jay Boyer. "The 'Snowball Approach' to Debt," Northwestern Kellogg School of Management. August 12, 2012. *www.kellogg.northwestern.edu/news_art icles/2012/snowball-approach.aspx*

20. Seth Godin. "Full Program Details," *Alt MBA. https:// altmba.com/info*

21. "Mike Rowe," Wikipedia. *https://en.wikipedia.org/ wiki/Mike_Rowe#Trade_activism*

22. "About the Foundation," mikeroweWORKS Foundation. *http://profoundlydisconnected.com/foundation/*

23. Josh Kaufman. *The Personal MBA: Master The Art of Business.* New York: Penguin Group, 2012.

24. Quotes About Planning. *Goodreads. www.goodreads. com/quotes/tag/planning*

Chapter 3

1. Peter Drucker. *GoodReads.com. www.goodreads.com/ author/quotes/12008.Peter_F_Drucker*

2. Michelle Brownstein. "Personal Capital's Affluent Investor Outlook 2018," *Personal Capital.* December 13, 2017. *www.personalcapital.com/blog/whitepapers/ investment-tax-giving-outlook-2018/*

3. Nate Nicholson. *How to Be Happy Every Single Day: 63 Proven Ways to Books Your Happiness and Live a More Positive Life.* New York: Blue Sky Publishing, 2014.

4. Joshua Becker. "21 Surprising Statistics that Reveal How Much Stuff We Actually Own," *Becoming Mini malist.www.becomingminimalist.com/clutter-stats/*

5. Marie Kondo. *The Life-Changing Magic of Tidying.* United Kingdom: Random House Publishing, 2014.

6. Richard Fry. "Millennials Surpass Gen Xers as the Largest Generation in U.S. Labor Force," Pew Research Center. May 11, 2015. *www.pewresearch.org/ fact-tank/2015/05/11/millennials-surpass-gen-xers -as-the-largest-generation-in-u-s-labor-force/*

7. Elizabeth Dunn and Michael Norton. *Happy Money: The Science of Happier Spending.* New York: Simon & Schuster, 2014.

8. Christine DiGangi. "The Class of 2016 Will Graduate With an Average of $37,172 in Debt," *Fox Business.* May 06, 2016. *www.foxbusiness.com/fea-*

*tures/2016/05/06/class-2016-will-graduate-with
-average-37172-in-debt.html*

9. Chris Weller and Andy Kiersz. "How Much Money Millennials Need to Earn to Be in the Top 1% at Every Age," *Business Insider.* August 9, 2017 *www.busi nessinsider.com/top-1-percent-income-for-millenni als-every-age-2017-8*

10. Philip Taylor. Interview with the author, December 7, 2017.

11. Ibid.

12. Ibid.

13. Nick Loper. Interview with the author, December 19, 2017.

14. Nicole Lapin. Nicolelapin.com. *https://nicolelapin. com/welcome/about-nicole-new/*

15. Nicole Lapin. *Rich Bitch: A Simple 12-Step Plan to for Getting Your Financial Like Together . . . Finally.* New York: HarperCollins Publishers, 2016.

16. Nicole Lapin. *Boss Bitch: A Simple 12-Step Plan to Take Charge of Your Career.* New York: Crown Business, 2017.

17. Collin Brennan. "Millennials Earn 20% Less than Boomers Did at Same Stage of Life," *USA Today.* January 13, 2017. *www.usatoday.com/story/mon ey/2017/01/13/millennials-falling-behind-boomer -parents/96530338/*

18. Brad Klontz. "Getting Sentimental Could Increase Your Savings," *Psychology Today.* October 12, 2017. *www.psychologytoday.com/blog/mind-over-mon ey/201710/getting-sentimental-could-increase-your -savings*

Chapter 4

1. David Landy, Noah Silbert, and Aleah Goldinc. "Estimating Large Numbers," *Cognitive Science: A Mult idisciplinary Journal.* August 12, 2012.

2. Kate Baggaley. "Why We Can't Grasp Very Large Numbers," *BrainDecoder.* October 23, 2015. *http://be hdad.org/mirror/www.braindecoder.com/happy-mole day-large-numbers-in-the-brain-1418905338.html*

3. Ibid.

4. Walter Mischel, Ebbe Ebbesen, and Antonette Zeiss. "Cognitive and Attentional Mechanisms in Delay of Gratification," *Journal of Personality and Social Psy chology.* 1972.

5. Ibid.

6. Ibid.

7. Ibid.

8. "Car Depreciation: 5 Things to Consider," *CarFax.* May 18, 2017. *www.carfax.com/blog/car-depreciation*

9. "Leasing vs. Buying a New Car," *Consumer Reports.* September 19, 2017. *www.consumerreports.org/ cro/2012/12/buying-vs-leasing-basics/index.htm*

10. Joann Muller. "What the Rich People Really Drive," *Forbes.* December 20, 2011. *www.forbes.com/sites/ joannmuller/2011/12/30/what-the-rich-people-really -drive/#569cb3301728*

11. Bela Gandhi. "6 Major Reasons Why People Get Divorced," *Today.* October 25, 2017. *www.today.com/ health/why-couples-get-divorced-t117476*

12. Erin Lowry. *The Broke Millennial: Stop Scraping by and Get Your Financial Life Together*. New York: TarcherPerigee, 2017.

13. *www.examiner.com/article/finances-remain-leading -cause-of-divorce*

14. Quentin Fottrel. "Most Americans Have Less than $1,000 in Savings," *MarketWatch*. December 23, 2015. *www.marketwatch.com/story/most-americans -have-less-than-1000-in-savings-2015-10-06*

15. Ron Lieber. "Money Talks to Have Before Marriage," *New York Times*. October 23, 2009. *www.nytimes. com/2009/10/24/your-money/24money.html?_r=2*

16. *Wall Street: Money Never Sleeps*. Twentieth Century Fox. 2010.

17. Maria Popova. "Seneca on Overcoming Fear and the Surest Strategy for Protecting Yourself from Misfortune," *BrainPickings.org*. *www.brainpickings. org/2016/02/15/seneca-letter-18/*

18. Andrew Francis and Hugo Mialon. "'A Diamond is Forever' and Other Fairy Tales: The Relationship between Wedding Expenses and Marriage Duration," *Emory University*. March 10, 2015. *file:///Users/con orrichardson/Downloads/SSRN-id2501480.pdf*

19. Lindsay Kolowich. "The Engagement Ring Story: How De Beers Created a Multi-Billion Dollar Industry From the Ground Up," *Hubspot,* July 28, 2017. *http://blog. hubspot.com/marketing/diamond-de-beers-marketing -campaign#sm.0001sm46ws4cdevxzmv1txwlmae2j*

20. Rohin Dhar. "Diamonds Are Bullshit," *Priceonom ics*. March 19, 2013. *http://blog.priceonomics.com/ post/45768546804/diamonds-are-bullshit*

21. Edward Epstein. "Have You Ever Tried to Sell A Diamond?" *The Atlantic*. February 1982. *www.theatlantic.com/magazine/archive/1982/02/have-you-ever-tried-to-sell-a-diamond/304575/?single_page=true*

22. Andrew Francis and Hugo Mialon. "'A Diamond is Forever' and Other Fairy Tales: The Relationship between Wedding Expenses and Marriage Duration," *Emory University*. March 10, 2015. *file:///Users/conorrichardson/Downloads/SSRN-id2501480.pdf*

23. Ivy Jacobson. "The National Average Costs of a Wedding is $32,641," *The Knot.com*. February 1982. *www.theknot.com/content/average-wedding-cost-2015*

24. Zaleski, Jessica. "How Long Is Too Long to Be Engaged?" TheKnot.com. *www.theknot.com/content/too-long-to-be-engaged*

25. Peter Thiel and Blake Masters. *Zero to One: Notes on Startups, or How to Build the Future*. New York: Crown Publishing House, 2014.

26. Eddy Ng. "Are Millennials More Likely to Switch Jobs and Employers," *Psychology Today*. March 29, 2015. *www.psychologytoday.com/blog/diverse-and-competitive/201503/are-millennials-more-likely-switch-jobs-and-employers*

27. Mona Chalabi. "How Many Times Does the Average Person Move?" *FiveThirtyEight.com*. January 29, 2015. *https://fivethirtyeight.com/features/how-many-times-the-average-person-moves/*

28. Diana Olick. "Is Homeownership Worth It? Not in These Cities," *CNBC*. February 04, 2016. *www.cnbc.com/2016/02/04/is-homeownership-worth-it-not-in-these-cities.html*

29. United States Census Bureau, The. "Monthly New Residential Sales, December 2017," *Census.gov*. January 25, 2018. *www.census.gov/construction/nrs/pdf/newressales.pdf*

30. Mortgage Calculator. Zillow. *www.zillow.com/mortgage-calculator/*

31. Tanza Loudenback. " Middle-Class Americans Made More Money Last Year than Ever Before," *Business Insider*. September 12, 2017. *www.businessinsider.com/us-census-median-income-2017-9*

32. Becca Stanek. "The Average 401(k) Balance by Age," *Smart Asset*. November 14, 2017. *https://smartasset.com/retirement/average-401k-balance-by-age*

33. United States Census Bureau, The. "Median and Average Sales Prices of New Homes Sold in United States." *https://www.census.gov/construction/nrs/pdf/uspriceann.pdf*

34. Jeffrey Sparshott. "Millennials Become the Biggest Generation in the U.S. Workforce," *Wall Street Journal*. March 15, 2015. *https://blogs.wsj.com/economics/2015/05/11/millennials-become-the-biggest-generation-in-the-u-s-workforce/*

35. Don Lee. "Why Millennials Are Staying Away from Homeownership Despite an Improving Economy," *Los Angeles Times*. March 01, 2016. *www.latimes.com/business/la-fi-0301-housing-economy-20160301-story.html*

36. United States Census Bureau, The. "Median and Average Sales Prices of New Homes Sold in United States." *https://www.census.gov/construction/nrs/pdf/uspriceann.pdf*

37. D'Vera Cohn, Jeffrey Passel, Wendy Wang, and Gretchen Livingston. "Barely Half of U.S. Adults Are Married—A Record Low," Pew Research Center. December 14, 2011. *www.pewsocialtrends.org/2011/12/14/ barely-half-of-u-s-adults-are-married-a-record-low/*

38. Dionne Searcy. "Most Americans Are Renting, and Paying More, as Homeownership Falls," *New York Times*. June 24, 2015. *www.nytimes.com/2015/06/24/ business/economy/more-americans-are-renting-and -paying-more-as-homeownership-falls.html?_r=0*

Chapter 5

1. Monique Morrissey. "The State of American Retirement: How 401(k)s Have Failed Most American Workers," Economic Policy Institute. March 03, 2016. *www.epi.org/publication/retirement-in-america/*

2. Daniel Gilbert. *Stumbling on Happiness*. New York: Random House, 2006.

3. Hal Hershfield, Daniel Goldstein, William Sharpe, Jesse Fox, Leo Yeykelis, Laura Carstensen, and Jeremy Bailenson. "Increasing Saving Behavior Through Age-Progressed Renderings of the Future Self," *Jour nal of Marketing Research*. November 2011. *http:// journals.ama.org/doi/abs/10.1509/jmkr.48.SPL. S23?code=amma-site.*

4. Ibid.

5. Stefan Agrigoroaei, Angela Lee-Attardo, and Margie Lachman. "Stress and Subjective Age: Those With Greater Financial Stress Look Older," *Research on Aging:*

Sage Journals. July 14, 2016. *http://journals.sagepub. com/doi/abs/10.1177/0164027516658502*

6. Thomas Kenny. "Stocks Vs. Bonds: The Long-Term Performance Data," *The Balance.* October 28, 2017. *www.multpl.com/10-year-treasury-rate/table/by-year*

7. Elyssa Kirkham. "1 in 3 Americans Has Saved $0 for Retirement," *Money.com.* March 14. 2016. *http://time. com/money/4258451/retirement-savings-survey/*

8. Ibid.

9. "Millennials Expect to Retire Earlier than Their Parents and Live Till They Are Just 79," *Blackrock.* November 11, 2015. *www.blackrock.com/corporate/ en-gb/newsroom/press-releases/article/corporate-one/ press-releases/millennials-expect-to-retire-earlier_GB*

10. Internal Revenue Service. "IRA FAQs—Distributions (Withdrawals)" IRS website. *www.irs.gov/retirement -plans/retirement-plans-faqs-regarding-iras-distribu tions-withdrawals*

11. Burton Malkiel. *A Random Walk Down Wall Street.* New York: W. W. Norton & Company; 9th ed., 2007.

Chapter 6

1. David Gelb. "Jiro Dreams of Sushi," *Independent Lens.* March 12, 2012. *www.imdb.com/title/tt1772925/*

2. "Robo-advisor," Wikipedia. *https://en.wikipedia.org/ wiki/Robo-advisor*

3. Mark Haefele, Simon Smiles, and Matthew Carter. "Millennials—the global guardians of capital," UBS. June 22, 2017. *https://www.ubs.com/global/en/wealth*

-management/chief-investment-office/our-research/
discover-more/2017/millennials.html

4. "A History of Robo-Advisors," *FutureAdvisor*. April 8, 2015. *https://www.futureadvisor.com/content/blog/ history-of-robo-advisors*

5. Jon Stein. "The History of Betterment: How We Started A Company That Changed An Industry," *Betterment*. July 20, 2016. *https://www.betterment.com/ resources/the-history-of-betterment/*

6. Peggy Collins. "Robo-Advisors," Bloomberg. June 6, 2017. https://www.bloomberg.com/quicktake/robo-advisers

7. Thomas Davenport, Barry Libert, and Megan Beck. "Robo-Advisors Are Coming to Consulting and Corporate Strategy," *Harvard Business Review*. January 12, 2018. *https://hbr.org/2018/01/robo-advisers-are -coming-to-consulting-and-corporate-strategy*

8. "Robo-Advisor Fee Comparison," *Value Penguin*.

9. Andrew Meola. "Is Robo-Advising Better than Traditional Investing? See the Pros and Cons," *Business Insider*. January 9, 2017. *www.businessinsider.com/4 -reasons-robo-investing-growing-2017-1*

10. Nicholas Yeap, Charles Paikert, and Suleman Din. "The Hard Truth About the Rise of Robo-Advisors," *Financial-Planning.com*. October 6, 2016. *www.fi nancial-planning.com/slideshow/the-hard-truth-about -the-rise-of-robo-advisors*

11. Arielle O'Shea and Anna-Louise Jackson. "Best Robo-Advisors: 2018 Top Picks," *NerdWallet*. January 9, 2018. *www.nerdwallet.com/blog/investing/best-robo -advisors/*

INDEX